Can America Afford to Grow Old?

Can America Afford to Grow Old?

Paying for Social Security

Henry J. Aaron
Barry P. Bosworth
Gary T. Burtless

The Brookings Institution
Washington, D.C.

Copyright © 1989 by
THE BROOKINGS INSTITUTION
1775 Massachusetts Avenue, N.W., Washington, D.C. 20036

9 8 7 6 5 4 3 2 1

The paper used in this publication meets the minimum
requirements of the American National Standard for Information
Sciences—Permanence of Paper for Printed Library Materials, ANSI
Z39.48-1984

Set in Caledonia with Helvetica display.
Composition by Monotype Composition,
*   Baltimore, Maryland*
Printing by Bookcrafters
*   Chelsea, Michigan*

THE BROOKINGS INSTITUTION

The Brookings Institution is an independent organization devoted to nonpartisan research, education, and publication in economics, government, foreign policy, and the social sciences generally. Its principal purposes are to aid in the development of sound public policies and to promote public understanding of issues of national importance.

The Institution was founded on December 8, 1927, to merge the activities of the Institute for Government Research, founded in 1916, the Institute of Economics, founded in 1922, and the Robert Brookings Graduate School of Economics and Government, founded in 1924.

The Board of Trustees is responsible for the general administration of the Institution, while the immediate direction of the policies, program, and staff is vested in the President, assisted by an advisory committee of the officers and staff. The by-laws of the Institution state: "It is the function of the Trustees to make possible the conduct of scientific research, and publication, under the most favorable conditions, and to safeguard the independence of the research staff in the pursuit of their studies and in the publication of the results of such studies. It is not a part of their function to determine, control, or influence the conduct of particular investigations or the conclusions reached."

The President bears final responsibility for the decision to publish a manuscript as a Brookings book. In reaching his judgment on the competence, accuracy, and objectivity of each study, the President is advised by the director of the appropriate research program and weighs the views of a panel of expert outside readers who report to him in confidence on the quality of the work. Publication of a work signifies that it is deemed a competent treatment worthy of public consideration but does not imply endorsement of conclusions or recommendations.

The Institution maintains its position of neutrality on issues of public policy in order to safeguard the intellectual freedom of the staff. Hence interpretations or conclusions in Brookings publications should be understood to be solely those of the authors and should not be attributed to the Institution, to its trustees, officers, or other staff members, or to the organizations that support its research.

Foreword

AFTER YEARS of relative obscurity, social security emerged in the 1970s as not only the largest but also one of the most controversial domestic programs of the federal government. The controversy concerned not social security benefits themselves, which have remained overwhelmingly popular with the American public, but the adequacy of revenue to ensure that promised benefits could be paid. Then in 1977 and 1983 financial crises led to legislation that cut benefits and raised revenues, ensuring the medium-term financial prospects of the social security system. Revenues are now projected to exceed outlays for many years, even under economic and demographic assumptions more pessimistic than most people expect.

Widespread concern remains, however, about the long-run prospect of the social security system. Will payment of currently promised pension and health benefits impose insupportable burdens on workers when the baby-boom generation starts to retire around 2010? Are currently legislated payroll taxes sufficient to pay for those benefits? Another concern is whether the social security trust funds should continue to be consolidated in the overall federal budget. At present the large and growing surpluses in those funds are concealing the true size of the budget deficit.

In this book Henry J. Aaron, Barry P. Bosworth, and Gary Burtless address these and other questions and conclude that workers in the future will indeed be required to shoulder greater burdens to meet the costs of currently promised benefits. But the size of those burdens will depend sensitively on future growth of labor productivity. They also find that if national saving is increased by the projected additions to social security reserves, the added national income that this capital accumulation will make possible will offset most of the added costs of the benefits. They therefore urge that the swelling social security surpluses be used not to offset deficits in other parts of the federal budget but to raise national saving.

The authors are senior fellows in the Brookings Economic Studies program. They are grateful to Robert M. Ball, Alan S. Blinder, Paul R. Cullinan, John C. Hambor, Robert W. Hartman, Selig D. Lesnoy,

Alicia H. Munnell, Robert J. Myers, William D. Nordhaus, Joseph A. Pechman, Rudy G. Penner, Robert D. Reischauer, and Charles L. Schultze for their helpful comments on various chapters. They also wish to thank Stephen Goss of the Social Security Administration for the data underlying the simulations presented in the text. Julie Gerber-Fields and Phyllis A. Arthur provided research assistance. Alice M. Carroll edited the manuscript, Victor M. Alfaro and Anna M. Nekoranec checked it for factual accuracy, and Florence Robinson prepared the index.

Research for this book was financed in part by a contract from the Social Security Administration. Brookings is grateful for that support.

The views expressed in this volume are those of the authors and should not be ascribed to the trustees, officers, or other staff members of the Brookings Institution or to the Social Security Administration.

BRUCE K. MACLAURY
President

November 1988
Washington, D.C.

Contents

Appendixes

Tables

Figures

CHAPTER 1

Introduction

RECENT LEGISLATION has dramatically changed U.S. policy toward social security reserves. From the mid-1950s through 1983, social security revenues approximately equaled annual expenditures. Small annual surpluses led to the accumulation of reserves that never amounted to more than a small percentage of national income. By 1988, however, annual social security and medicare surpluses had grown beyond $50 billion. In 1988 dollars the surpluses are projected to swell to more than $100 billion by the mid-1990s, reach more than $175 billion in 2010, and cumulate to over $2 trillion in the next century.

How to use the social security surpluses is a critical question facing the United States. They can be set aside to boost national saving and thereby help finance the future costs of a large retired population. Alternatively, the United States could simply consume the surpluses, using them to offset deficits in other federal programs.

If current and projected social security and medicare surpluses are included in the federal budget, the deficit appears to be declining and may well vanish during the mid- to late 1990s even without further spending cuts or tax increases. When the social insurance surpluses are excluded, however, the deficit not only appears larger but is projected to increase. The difference between the deficit inclusive of social security and medicare and the deficit exclusive of these programs will grow progressively larger.

We believe that superior fiscal policy will result if deficit-reduction targets are set excluding social security and medicare. Social security and medicare represent obligations to pay large future benefits. Future generations of workers will have to produce the goods and services needed to redeem those claims. The only way to help those workers bear that burden is to help them to increase the incomes they can earn. The accumulation of reserves in the social insurance system can help achieve that goal but can do so only if these reserves increase national saving, add to the capital stock, and thereby raise future incomes. Pursuing such a policy will relieve future workers of any added burden from social security benefits for the large baby-

1

boom generation. Furthermore, it will meet most of the added burden
of increased medicare hospital benefits. Deficit targets defined in
terms of a budget that excludes the retirement accounts will increase
the likelihood that the additions to reserves will raise national saving.

By our definition, the budget deficit now is considerably larger
than the deficit in the consolidated budget accounts used by the
Congressional Budget Office and the Office of Management and
Budget. Eliminating the non-social-insurance deficit or reducing it to
less than, say, 1 percent of gross national product is a far more
ambitious target than the deficit-reduction targets adopted in the
Balanced Budget Act of 1985, which calls only for budget balance
including the social insurance surpluses.

Baby Boom, Baby Bust

The average age of Americans is rising. The decline in birth rates
and the rise in longevity have raised the median age in the population
by four years since 1970, from twenty-eight to thirty-two.[1] This
demographic trend is not unique to the United States. All developed
countries have experienced declining birth and death rates over the
past century.[2]

The United States is unusual, however, for the magnitude of its
demographic swings in recent years. Birth rates rose sharply after
World War II, generating what is known as the "baby boom"; they
reached a maximum during the period from 1955 through 1959 and
then fell sharply.[3] As a result, the proportion of children in the U.S.
population rose and then fell. The proportion over sixty-four years
old has risen continuously (table 1-1). Under current projections that
share of the population will continue to rise slowly until 2008 and
then rapidly over the following three decades as the baby-boom
generation retires. The fraction of the population that is elderly will
remain far above current levels indefinitely unless birth rates rise
significantly.

1. U.S. Bureau of the Census, *Statistical Abstract of the United States, 1988*
(Government Printing Office, 1987), p. 13.
2. See Peter S. Heller, Richard Hemming, and Peter W. Kohnert, *Aging and
Social Expenditure in the Major Industrial Countries, 1980–2025*, Occasional Paper
47 (Washington, D.C.: International Monetary Fund, 1986).
3. The total fertility rate necessary to maintain the population, assuming no net
immigration, is about 2.1 children per woman. The total fertility rate averaged 3.69
from 1955 through 1959. It fell to 1.74 in 1976. It was 1.87 in 1987.

TABLE 1-1. **Ratio of Younger and Older Populations to Population Aged Twenty to Sixty-four, Selected Years, 1950–2060**

	Ratio to twenty- to sixty-four-year-olds		
Year	Under twenty-year-olds	Over sixty-four-year-olds	Under twenty-plus over sixty-four-year-olds
1950	0.581	0.138	0.719
1960	0.731	0.173	0.904
1965	0.764	0.182	0.946
1970	0.715	0.185	0.900
1975	0.642	0.189	0.832
1980	0.558	0.195	0.753
1985	0.505	0.200	0.704
1990	0.485	0.210	0.695
2000	0.458	0.215	0.673
2010	0.411	0.223	0.633
2020	0.411	0.292	0.703
2030	0.423	0.378	0.801
2040	0.415	0.391	0.806
2050	0.416	0.397	0.813
2060	0.418	0.412	0.830

Source: *1988 Annual Report of the Board of Trustees of the Federal Old-Age and Survivors Insurance and Disability Insurance Trust Funds* (Baltimore, Md.: Social Security Administration, 1988), table A-1, p. 93. Projections for 1990–2060 based on alternative II-B assumptions.

These population trends mean that the elderly will consume a growing proportion of total output if their living standards remain similar to those of the rest of the population. For the retired elderly, consumption must be financed by some combination of private and public pensions and private savings. All of this consumption will come from the output of active workers.

Burdens of an Aging Population

Will the future consumption of the elderly severely burden future workers? To what extent can policies undertaken today reduce those burdens?

These questions do not arise, of course, if the elderly work. The working elderly pay for their consumption largely out of current earnings, which approximate the value of their contribution to current output. Nor will the questions arise if retirees pay for consumption out of their own savings. By forgoing consumption when they were young, the elderly will have increased investment through their savings, contributed to the growth of the capital stock, and added to productivity. By using their savings to support consumption once they have retired, the elderly simply reclaim the consumption they voluntarily deferred. Similarly, the consumption financed out of fully funded private pensions represents deferred consumption. In this case, the saving is carried out collectively through the reserves set aside out of contributions by employers and employees. But in no case is it legitimate to fear that the elderly will burden the young.

↗Consumption of the elderly financed through public programs that provide cash or in-kind benefits may, however, impose burdens on active workers↝ If beneficiaries of these programs paid taxes only sufficient to pay for the current services government provided them when they were young, then any additional services in cash or in kind that they receive when old represent burdens on current workers. The programs would not impose burdens on active workers if the beneficiaries had previously paid taxes in excess of the value of public services they consumed. These extra taxes would add to the government's budget surplus or reduce its deficit, in either case adding to national saving, much as do private saving or the reserves set aside to pay for future pension obligations. Government budget surpluses add to national saving to the same extent as does private saving.

This book attempts to determine the size of the burdens that social security and medicare hospital insurance will impose on future workers and to evaluate the actions that can be taken today to reduce or eliminate these burdens.

Perceptions of Social Security and Medicare

A full examination of the costs of services for the elderly and disabled would require a comprehensive examination of all programs that serve these groups. This book focuses on the two largest programs—social security and part A of medicare. These programs, known collectively as old-age, survivors, disability, and hospital insurance, or OASDHI, account for most of current federal expenditures on the elderly and disabled. They are the only programs for which long-term cost estimates are made.

Financial Projections

The OASDHI programs have been the subject of intense debate and considerable confusion. The public confusion is regrettable, but understandable. In part it reflects important shifts in the financial condition of the programs. In 1972 the old-age, survivors, and disability insurance (OASDI) portions of the system were believed to be so securely funded that Congress raised benefits 20 percent and provided for automatic adjustments for inflation but legislated only modest increases in the dedicated payroll taxes used to finance these benefits. When these reforms were complete, the social security actuaries certified that revenues were sufficient to pay for benefits over the next seventy-five years. Before the end of the 1970s, however, and again in the early 1980s, large deficits emerged and threatened the financial viability of the social security system. The deficits, caused principally by slowing economic growth and falling birth rates, prompted Congress to enact benefit cuts and tax increases in 1977 and again in 1983. Hospital insurance (HI) was only added to the benefits program in 1965. In 1982 official projections indicated that the hospital insurance system would exhaust its reserves by 1988. But by 1988 hospital insurance reserves were projected to be sufficient to carry the program through 2005.[4]

As the 1980s come to a close, conflicting reports on the condition of old-age, survivors, and disability insurance abound. Some observers recognize that social security is running large and growing surpluses. Others claim that rapid growth of social security benefits is to blame for part of the current federal deficit. And still others express concern that future growth of social security benefits will become a serious drag on the growth of consumption of American workers.

The Policy Context

In part, changing views of social security and medicare reflect real changes over the last two decades in the economy and the federal budget. From the end of World War II until 1973 the United States economy grew rapidly. National income per person employed grew 70 percent, an average annual rate of 2.1 percent from 1948 through 1973, and fertility rates were well above prewar levels. But by the end of the 1970s both trends had shifted. Growth of national income per person employed slowed to just 0.4 percent per year from 1973 through 1987.[5] And birth rates, which had gone above prewar levels

4. *1988 Annual Report of the Board of Trustees of the Federal Old-Age and Survivors Insurance and Disability Insurance [OASDI] Trust Funds* (Baltimore, Md.: Social Security Administration, 1988), p. 12.
   5. Ibid., p. 33.

TABLE 1-2. **Net Saving and Investment in the United States as a Share of Net National Product, 1951–87**

Percent of net national product

Year	Private saving[a]	+	Govern-ment saving	=	National saving	=	Net domestic invest-ment	+	Net foreign invest-ment
1951–60	8.7		−0.7		8.0		7.7		0.3
1961–70	9.4		−1.0		8.4		7.7		0.7
1971–80	9.7		−2.0		7.7		7.5		0.3
1981–85	8.2		−4.5		3.7		5.0		−1.3
1986	7.2		−5.2		2.0		5.7		−3.8
1987	6.1		−4.1		2.0		5.8		−3.8

Source: U.S. Department of Commerce, Bureau of Economic Analysis, *National Income and Product Accounts of the United States, 1929–82: Statistical Tables* (Government Printing Office, 1986); and *Survey of Current Business,* various issues. Net saving and investment equal the gross flow minus capital consumption allowances (the depreciation of existing capital). Net national product equals gross national product minus capital consumption allowances.

a. Business and household saving. Employee pension funds of state and local governments are allocated to household saving to match the treatment of private pension funds.

in the late 1950s, have now fallen below those needed to maintain a constant population.

These trends make a difference in how social security is viewed because the tax rate necessary to pay for a given package of benefits is inversely related to the growth of productivity and of the work force. Thus, the declines in economic growth and fertility have increased the price of social security benefits to American workers. An important change in the economic environment that affects attitudes toward OASDHI financing is the collapse of U.S. national saving, part of which is attributable to the emergence of large and intractable federal budget deficits. National saving is the sum of private saving and the government surplus. When the government budget is in deficit, national saving is smaller than private saving. The government budget deficit or surplus consists of the OASDHI balance plus the surplus or deficit in other government programs.

Over the last two decades, three important shifts in these quantities have occurred. The government deficit has risen sharply—from an average 1.0 percent of net national product from 1948 through 1980 to an average 5.1 percent from 1981 through 1987. Private saving, which averaged 8.7 percent of net national product in the 1950s, 9.4 percent during the 1960s, and 9.7 percent during the 1970s, had fallen to an average of 6.6 percent in 1986 and 1987. Both trends have contributed to a sharp drop in U.S. national saving (table 1-2).

The third shift, in the financial position of social security and

TABLE 1-3. **Role of the Social Security and Medicare Trust Funds in the Federal Budget Surplus or Deficit, Selected Fiscal Years, 1980–94**

Billions of dollars

		Surplus or deficit		
Year	Total budget	HI[a]	OASDI[b]	Non-OASDHI
1980	−74	1	−1	−74
1987	−150	12	20	−182
1988	−155	16	39	−210
1994	−121	14	113	−248
Change				
1980–88	−81	15	40	−136
1988–94	34	−2	74	−38

Source: *Historical Tables: Budget of the United States Government, Fiscal Year 1989*, pp. 16, 313, and 317 for fiscal 1980 and 1987; and Congressional Budget Office, *The Economic Outlook: An Update* (CBO, August 1988), p. 60 for fiscal 1988–94.
 a. Hospital insurance.
 b. Old-age, survivors, and disability insurance.

medicare hospital insurance, has given these programs a crucial role in the overall budget. The OASDHI system is beginning to run large annual surpluses, which in the total budget are masking deficits in other government operations that are even larger than the overall deficits indicate.

At present, the federal government sets budget targets based on total revenues and spending, with OASDHI surpluses offsetting deficits on other operations. The growing surpluses in the social security system camouflage a major deterioration in the budget balance for non-OASDHI operations. As table 1-3 shows, the total federal budget deficit rose an estimated $81 billion between 1980 and 1988 but is projected to fall $34 billion between 1988 and 1994. The total deficit in 1994 is projected to be a relatively manageable $121 billion— roughly 2 percent of gross national product. Because the total deficit is declining, some observers have argued that the budget deficit problem is behind us, implying for conservatives that no tax increase is required and for liberals that the government can now afford to undertake new programs.

But the non-OASDHI deficit in 1994 is projected at $248 billion, or over 4 percent of gross national product. In effect, the current policy is to borrow the OASDHI surplus to finance a deficit in the rest of the budget. As a result the payroll tax, ostensibly earmarked for retirement, survivors, disability, and hospital insurance, is being used increasingly to pay for other government expenditures, such as defense and interest on the public debt. Because the payroll tax excludes all capital income and labor income above the social security taxable wage ceiling, the use of the payroll tax rather than personal and corporation income taxes to pay for ordinary government services implies a significant shift in the distribution of tax burdens from upper- to lower-income taxpayers.

Changing Perspectives

In the past two decades views concerning the linkage between financing and distribution of the benefits of the OASDHI programs have changed. These programs can be viewed as a tax and transfer system in which one group—workers—is taxed to pay for benefits received currently by other groups—retirees, survivors, and disabled beneficiaries. Or they can be regarded as a retirement system in which workers pay taxes during their working lives in return for benefits they themselves or their families receive as retirees, survivors, or disabled persons.

The first view focuses on OASDHI revenues and expenditures at a particular point in time. It ignores the fact that people typically work and pay taxes and later receive cash payments or benefits in kind.[6] The second view focuses on the life-cycle experience with OASDHI of a single worker or cohort of workers. It ignores the fact that at each instant taxes are being imposed on one group in the population to cover the cost of benefits for another. Both views ignore the family bonds or other connections that often link the young and the old, the active and the disabled.

The life-cycle view has come to dominate analyses of the social security system.[7] Few persons would apply the tax-transfer perspective to private pensions, since that would suggest that active workers are forgoing consumption so that current retirees can receive pensions. Recognizing that workers save, individually or collectively, to provide for their own subsequent benefits, most analysts find it reasonable to

6. For an expression of this view, see Joseph A. Pechman, Henry J. Aaron, and Michael K. Taussig, *Social Security: Perspectives for Reform* (Brookings, 1968).

7. For expressions of this view, see Martin Feldstein, "Social Security, Induced Retirement, and Aggregate Capital Accumulation," *Journal of Political Economy*, vol. 82 (September–October 1974), pp. 905–26; Henry J. Aaron, *The Economic Effects of Social Security* (Brookings, 1982); and B. Douglas Bernheim, "The Economic Effects of Social Security: Toward a Reconciliation of Theory and Measurement," *Journal of Public Economics*, vol. 33 (August 1987), pp. 273–304.

apply the same perspective to public pensions that is applied to private pensions.

Under the tax-transfer view, annual surpluses and reserves in the OASDHI fund—beyond the amounts necessary to forestall forced tax increases at inconvenient times such as during a recession—have little rationale. Under the life-cycle view, the accumulation of reserves seems natural, just as it is for private pensions. Each worker or cohort of workers is seen as paying taxes that approximate the actuarial value of the benefits the workers or cohort will eventually receive.

The attitude among economists toward the desirability of increasing national saving has also shifted. Keynesian economic analysis viewed saving in any form with some ambivalence. On the one hand, net saving was necessary if a country was to increase its capital stock. On the other hand, saving threatened full employment because it represented a decision not to spend. If saving exceeded investment requirements, total spending might be insufficient to provide a market for all of the goods and services that could be produced at full employment. The result, it was feared, would be recession.

While recessions still occur, economists increasingly are persuaded that well-timed use of monetary policy and induced adjustments in investment and international trade balances are capable of generating sufficient demand by domestic and foreign households and businesses to maintain full employment at a wide variety of national saving rates. Fears of excessive saving in the United States seem fanciful in light of saving rates now far below current U.S. domestic investment. Instead, a dearth of saving is widely seen as a threat to long-term economic growth.

Financing Social Security and Medicare

Running annual surpluses and accumulating a large trust fund reflect a major shift in social security policy. From the early 1950s until recently, Congress set OASDHI payroll tax rates so that revenues would approximately equal outlays. Under such pay-as-you-go financing, workers each year paid enough in taxes to cover the cost of current benefits. In return, they anticipated similar support during their own retirement years from taxes on future workers. If the ratio of beneficiaries to active workers and the rate of growth of real wages remain constant, each generation of workers except the first will end up getting benefits that bear the same relation to the taxes they have paid as will every other generation. The first generation of recipients obviously receives benefits without major tax costs.[8]

The pay-as-you-go system contrasts with a funded system in which workers or worker cohorts receive in benefits only what they have paid in tax, plus interest earnings on those payments. A funded system leads to the accumulation of sizable reserves; a pay-as-you-go system does not. Moreover, those who retire soon after the introduction of any pension system would receive little if their benefits were tied to the taxes they have paid.

With the social security amendments of 1977 and 1983, Congress abandoned strict pay-as-you-go financing. By setting tax rates to yield more than projected costs for many years, Congress adopted policies leading to the accumulation of sizable reserves. These amendments required the large baby-boom cohorts to pay more in payroll taxes than would have been required to cover the costs of transfers to the relatively small cohorts of current beneficiaries. Viewed in life-cycle terms, however, the tax rates approximately equaled those necessary to cover the costs of the benefits the baby-boom cohorts would eventually receive.

The accumulation of reserves also means that payroll tax rates necessary when the baby-boom generation retires can be held below those necessary under pay-as-you-go financing. By keeping payroll tax rates down, such a policy appears to spare future workers some of the costs for benefits that they would otherwise have been asked to bear.

This appearance may be misleading, however. The consumption made possible by social security benefits in any future year will come out of goods and services produced at that time. Unless total production is increased enough to cover the added consumption by increased numbers of beneficiaries, future workers will suffer reduced consumption, or investment will be curtailed. The central question regarding the financing of social security and medicare is whether to try to use their reserves to increase national saving today, thereby adding to the stock of capital and to productive capacity, so that future output rises at least as much as will the cost of OASDHI benefits.

8. Because Congress has repeatedly increased social security benefits, few current beneficiaries have spent their entire working lives paying taxes sufficient to cover the costs of the current set of benefits. Even after allowing for the effects of inflation, current workers are paying and future workers will pay taxes much higher in relation to the benefits they will receive than current beneficiaries had to pay.

The answer to this question hinges on the answers to two other questions. How much should OASDHI revenues exceed annual spending? And how should targets be set for balance in the rest of the federal budget? Three broad courses are available.

First, if OASDHI revenues exceed annual expenditures, the resulting surpluses may be used to pay for current public or private consumption (either through increases in non-OASDHI government expenditures or through reductions in non-OASDHI taxes). As the OASDHI surpluses increase, so would deficits elsewhere in the federal budget. Although this policy may seem peculiar, it closely resembles the course on which the United States is embarked today. Under this policy, the reserve does not add to national saving (because it does not reduce the overall government budget deficit) and, hence, it does not add to future productive capacity. In effect, the OASDHI surpluses are borrowed to pay for current government services, replacing income tax revenues or cuts in other government programs sufficient to balance the non-OASDHI budget.

While such a policy might hold down future payroll tax rates, it cannot protect future taxpayers from shouldering the expense of rising benefit costs. When and if the trust funds are drawn down to pay for future benefits, other federal taxes will have to be increased to finance the repurchase of government debt previously bought by the OASDHI trust funds. In addition, the incomes against which those taxes are imposed will be no larger than if the reserve had never existed. Since future benefits must be paid out of future production, the burden on future taxpayers would not be reduced.

As a second option, the nation could abandon its current policy of accumulating large and sustained social security surpluses. In that event, social security revenues would be set roughly equal to annual expenditures.[9] No attempt would be made to use OASDHI financing to add to national saving. Any additional costs of social security and medicare resulting from benefits that would have to be provided for an enlarged population of beneficiaries would be met in the future by raising payroll taxes. As in the first financing alternative, national saving would be unaffected by the financing of OASDHI. Such a pay-as-you-go policy has obvious attractions for current workers, whose

---

9. Surpluses are necessary for a few years to build up a reserve adequate to tide social security over temporary shortfalls in revenues below projections. Such a reserve will be reached during the 1990s.

payroll taxes would be lower than those scheduled under current law over the next couple of decades.

Under the third alternative, OASDHI revenues would be kept above annual expenditures for an extended period, and the resulting reserve would be used to increase national saving and capital formation. In that case, current workers for many years would pay more taxes than necessary to cover the costs of OASDHI benefits and other government activities. As a result, their disposable incomes and presumably their consumption would be initially reduced to increase saving, raise the rate of growth in the stock of capital, and boost future production. The growth of economic capacity would be higher than if saving had not been increased. This added production could be used to cover part or all of the increased costs of OASDHI benefits. Pursuing the third alternative requires sustained surpluses and a termination of the current practice, illustrated in table 1-3, of using OASDHI reserves to pay for large and growing deficits elsewhere in the federal budget.

Examining the Effects of Alternative Policies

This book examines the economic consequences of each of the three alternatives for financing social security. Chapter 2 describes the current U.S. social insurance system—the ways in which benefits are earned, individual entitlements are calculated, and benefits are financed. It traces recent changes in the budget accounting of social security and medicare hospital insurance. It also examines the role of OASDHI benefits in improving the relative economic standing of the aged.

Chapter 3 describes the techniques used to determine whether Congress has set tax rates high enough to pay for promised benefits. It defines the concept of close actuarial balance and the role it plays in setting tax rates. This chapter also explains the key role in the cost estimates played by assumptions regarding future birth and mortality rates, productivity growth, and the real interest rate. It presents the results of current projections of the social security and medicare actuaries. Current law calls for combined employer and employee contributions to remain at 15.3 percent of taxable payroll after 1990.[10]

10. *1988 OASDI Annual Report*, p. 13.

The annual social security balance will turn negative around 2030 and the reserve will be exhausted around 2050, according to 1988 projections.[11] If current benefits are to be sustained and the balance between long-term revenues and expenditures is to be maintained, some increase in payroll tax rates will be necessary.

Our calculations indicate that if payroll tax rates are increased as soon as any long-run deficit emerges and the demographic and economic assumptions of the social security and medicare actuaries continue to hold, social security tax rates will have to be increased in several stages by a cumulative 2.4 percentage points between 1990 and 2060 to meet benefit obligations under current law. The future costs of medicare hospital insurance will add an additional 4.5 percentage points to the payroll tax. The size of the increases depends on economic and demographic assumptions, on the timing of the increases, and of course on the assumption that the benefit formulas remain unchanged.

Chapter 4 describes a model of the economy and of the social security system that we used to analyze the effects on the economy of different methods of financing social security and medicare hospital benefits. The model employs a large number of equations and accounting identities to represent the economy and the structure of social security costs and revenues. It provides baseline estimates of production, saving, taxes, and benefits, computed from assumptions used by the social security actuaries in preparing their 1986 projections, against which the effects of various financing policies can be judged. Because the model rests on well-tested economic theory, we have reasonable confidence in the general accuracy of our estimates of the differential effects of alternative policies. In contrast, we have no reason to think that the projections of the actual level of economic activity, which depend sensitively on countless variables that no one can accurately forecast, are any more than generally suggestive of what in fact will happen.

Chapter 5 projects the costs of providing benefits under a variety of assumptions about economic policy, including the use of social security surpluses to increase national saving. The economic burden of paying for social security when the baby-boom generation retires will add 1.8 percent to the 5.3 percent of net national product that

11. Ibid., pp. 141–42.

social security benefits now cost. The increase will be spread out over the years from 2005 to 2035. Between now and 2005 the share of net national product absorbed by social security will actually fall.

If national saving and domestic investment are increased by the additions to social security reserves, wages will rise about 7 percent more than trend growth. That increase would pay for the added pension costs generated by the rising proportion of beneficiaries in the total population. Workers active during the twenty-first century would actually enjoy a higher standard of living than in a world where the proportion of pensioners did not increase. The central question is whether social security surpluses will be used to add to national saving or to finance current consumption.

The cost of medicare hospital insurance is projected to rise not only because of increases in the proportion of aged and disabled beneficiaries in the total population, but also because the per capita cost of hospital care is expected to rise more rapidly than per capita earnings. Paying for these increased costs through pay-as-you-go financing will reduce the consumption of future active workers by as much as 4 percent by 2035 relative to what it otherwise would have been. However, currently legislated taxes are not high enough to pay for benefits to which the aged and disabled will be entitled under current law. If these costs are met instead by reducing future national saving—that is, through deficit financing—consumption would be affected less in the short run, but annual consumption of active workers would be reduced more in the long run because of the additional loss of capital that follows from a lower rate of saving.

The projected deficits in the hospital insurance system are so large that repeated tax increases will be needed to meet current obligations. If the tax increases are imposed in anticipation of the increase in benefit outlays, the hospital insurance trust fund will grow much larger than is expected under current law. If the combined reserves of social security and medicare add to national saving, the additions to capital and the associated increases in national income will raise the consumption possibilities of workers for most of the first three decades of the next century relative to what they would have been. The reduction in consumption in later years will be limited to roughly 1.2 percent. These projections in chapter 5 indicate that it is crucially important whether the reserves are used to add to U.S. national saving or are spent on current public and private consumption. Debates on the size and structure of social security, however, should not begin with exaggerated fears ("How will we cope?"), but with a reasoned examination of what role the elderly should play in the economy and society and how the social insurance system can help encourage such a role.

Chapter 6 examines the way in which social security reserves are invested and indicates the probable effects of several alternative policies. This chapter also addresses fears that social security reserves will be so large that they will be sufficient to buy up the national debt. It indicates what could be done if this possibility is realized. Public debt totaled $2 trillion at the end of 1987. Under current law, reserves of the old-age, survivors, and disability insurance systems are projected to top out at $12.8 trillion in about 2030 ($2 trillion in 1988 dollars). In the unlikely event that deficits on all operations other than social security ceased immediately or declined to modest levels, social security might indeed have enough assets to buy up the entire outstanding national debt. At recent rates of increase the overall debt of the government will far exceed the reserves of social security even at their peak. However, in our simulations that allow OASDHI reserves to add to saving, we assume that the rest of government operations will run an annual deficit of 1.5 percent of gross national product, about the historical average. In this case, the reserves of the OASDHI system will exceed the total government debt for extended periods.

We show in chapter 6 that even if social security absorbed most of the outstanding debt, the effects on the structure of interest rates would be small. The ability of the Federal Reserve System to carry out monetary policy would be unaffected. And even if reserves come to exceed outstanding government debt, a variety of alternative secure investments is available. The choice of assets in which to hold social security reserves will have little effect on U.S. economic growth because growth depends on the quality of business management and on real investments in plant, equipment, inventories, housing, education, and scientific research, not on which members of society happen to hold which kinds of financial securities. Investing reserves in assets that yield higher returns than the current portfolio would reduce the taxes needed to pay for any given set of benefits. Such a reallocation of financial assets would affect economic growth only if it led to the selection of higher productivity investments.

The concluding chapter examines the argument that individuals and the nation could reduce the burden of paying for retirement, survivors, and disability benefits if these systems were shifted from the public to the private sector. Privatization would raise the question of whether certain classes of beneficiaries, such as those with a history of low earnings or those who are part of large families, should continue to receive especially generous benefits relative to taxes paid. Privatization would require either that such assistance cease and that benefits be strictly proportional to earnings or that such households undergo income or means testing as a condition for aid. Chapter 7 shows that the effects of privatization on the real burdens of caring for the aged are likely to be negligible.

We conclude in chapter 7 that the question of whether OASDHI expenditures and revenues should be included with the rest of government operations in measuring the federal deficit or surplus is important only to the extent that it influences decisions affecting the size of the deficit or surplus. The recent decision to build up a large surplus in the social security system has created an opportunity to use the surpluses to boost national saving. Under current law, taxes are insufficient to build up such a reserve for medicare hospital insurance.[12] Use of reserves can boost the future consumption possibilities of active workers by about as much as the aging of the population will add to the future costs of benefit payments. The increases in capital formation that would produce this result can occur in the private or the public sector.

We express no view on whether any additions to saving that might result from the financing of social security and medicare should be used to finance private or public investment. The calculations we present in chapter 5 are based on an increase in private investment, most of which occurs in the nonfarm business sector. An increase in public investment—for example in bridges, highways, or education and training—would require independent justification. If such a case were made, it would provide a basis for running larger deficits on government activities than those used in our estimates.

Whether a problem is viewed as large or small always depends on the perspective of the observer. Our calculations indicate that OASDHI costs may have small positive or negative effects on the consumption possibilities of nonbeneficiaries for the next seventy-five years. The

---

12. Medicare taxes roughly track benefits for about the next decade and fall increasingly below benefits thereafter. The same rationale applies also to other programs that provide benefits for the aged and disabled, such as medicare part B benefits for physicians' and other services. We are not examining these programs, however.

effects of the social security system alone will be positive if, through overall fiscal policies, social security reserves add to national saving; otherwise, the effects will be negative. The stakes in building up reserves for medicare hospital benefits and using these reserves to increase national saving are somewhat larger. But in no case will the effects be as large as those of even very small changes in the rate of growth of technical change, the work week, or labor force participation.

CHAPTER 2

The Social Security and Medicare Programs

SOCIAL SECURITY and medicare consist of four separate programs: old-age and survivors insurance (OASI), disability insurance (DI), hospital insurance (HI), and supplementary medical insurance (SMI). This volume focuses on the financing of old-age and survivors insurance, disability insurance, and hospital insurance, the three programs that are paid for largely with an earmarked payroll tax collected from wage earners, their employers, and the self-employed. Payroll taxes that finance the three programs are imposed on the earnings of almost 95 percent of all workers in the United States. Together with SMI, these programs provide benefits to one American in six and account for over one-quarter of total federal spending, or slightly more than $280 billion in 1987.

Historical Background

The Social Security Act of 1935 established old-age insurance as a contributory pension scheme for wage earners employed in commerce and industry. The initial plan established the principle, never since abandoned, that covered workers become insured under social security by accumulating earnings credits based on the duration of their employment in jobs covered by social security.[1] Starting in 1940, insured, retired sixty-five-year-olds were eligible for an old-age pension based on their earnings in covered employment, not on taxes paid. The fact that eligibility and benefits are based on earnings rather than on tax payments has important implications for the financing of social security pensions.

When first established, old-age insurance covered about 60 percent of U.S. workers. Subsequent extensions of coverage—to agricultural and domestic workers, the self-employed (including farmers), em-

1. For the history and the legal and administrative background of social security and medicare, see Robert J. Myers, *Social Security*, 3d ed. (Irwin, 1985).

ployees of public and nonprofit organizations (including most state and local governments), and federal government workers hired after 1983—have brought just over 92 percent of civilian workers under OASDI.[2] The percentage is expected to rise gradually as federal government workers increasingly become covered.

Social security benefits were liberalized even before the first monthly benefit checks were sent out. In 1939 Congress authorized payment of benefits to spouses and dependent children of retired workers and extended benefits to dependents of deceased covered workers and retirees, thus changing old-age insurance into old-age and survivors insurance (OASI). The 1939 amendments brought about the first of many revisions in the basic benefit formula, most of which served just to keep social security benefits approximately current with rising wages and prices. Without such adjustments the ratio of initial benefits to the average wage (the replacement rate) would have fallen, and inflation would have eroded the real value of benefits. In fact, periodic amendments did more than merely protect the real value of pensions for new beneficiaries; the replacement rate for a new retiree with average wages rose over time, from 31 percent in 1953 to 36 percent in 1971.[3]

In 1972 Congress increased benefits by one-fifth and introduced new rules that automatically adjusted benefits to reflect price increases. Because of technical errors in the indexing formula, new benefit awards rose more rapidly than warranted, either by wage growth or by price inflation. Congress corrected the error in 1977, but not in time to prevent replacement rates from rising to 51 percent in 1981.[4] The 1977 social security amendments trimmed replacement rates to 41 percent, the long-run target replacement rate for average-wage workers.[5]

2. Two of the principal uncovered groups are employees of certain state and local governments which have declined to become covered under social security and federal government workers hired before January 1984. Most of the latter have chosen to remain in the Civil Service Retirement program rather than become covered under social security. Members of the armed forces are covered by social security, and railroad employees covered by the Railroad Retirement program are in effect also covered as a result of the close links between the two programs.

3. Reported replacement rates are based solely on workers' pensions; spouses' and dependents' benefits are not considered. Robert J. Myers, *Summary of the Provisions of the OASDI System, the HI System, and the SMI System* (Washington, D.C.: Mercer Meidinger Hansen, 1988), p. 37.

4. Ibid.

5. Some retirees who became eligible during the phase-in period after the 1977

In 1956 Congress broadened social security by adding benefits for insured workers fifty or older who became disabled before retirement. Amendments in 1958 and 1960 removed the age limit and extended benefits to dependents of disabled workers. In 1965 Congress enacted medicare, a two-part program consisting of hospital insurance (HI, also known as medicare part A) and supplementary medical insurance (SMI, known as part B) which helps pay for physicians' services, laboratory and other diagnostic tests, and small amounts of home health care.

Congress originally extended HI eligibility only to people over sixty-five. Later, it extended benefits to recipients of disability insurance (though not their dependents) after a two-and-one-half-year period of disability. People over sixty-five who have not become insured under social security can obtain HI coverage for a monthly premium that approximately reflects the full actuarial cost of the program. In addition, medicare pays for dialysis and kidney transplants for victims of end-stage renal disease, regardless of age.

Alone among the main social insurance programs, supplementary medical insurance is voluntary. All Americans over sixty-five, whether or not they are eligible for other social security benefits, may buy coverage under SMI for a monthly premium that in 1967 covered about half of the costs and currently pays about a quarter. General federal revenues cover remaining costs of the program.

Financing

Social security and hospital insurance benefits have always been financed largely through a payroll tax imposed on covered workers and their employers.[6] Table 2-1 shows the payroll tax rates imposed

---

correction complained that they were being shortchanged. This group, born after 1916 and before 1922, is frequently referred to as notch babies. They actually qualify for higher replacement rates than Congress had intended in 1972, and higher rates in some cases than those available to workers born after 1921. But they receive lower benefits than people born just before them because the corrected formulas apply only to people born after 1916. The surge in replacement rates for people working until age sixty-five is illustrated in table 2-4, where rates for average-wage and high-wage workers are shown to rise sharply in the late 1970s and then fall sharply in the early 1980s.

6. A slightly larger percentage of the work force is covered by the HI payroll tax than the OASDI tax, however. All federal government workers are covered by the HI tax, although few of them are now covered by the OASDI tax. Workers covered by the Railroad Retirement system, in essence, also pay the HI tax, although in a somewhat indirect way.

TABLE 2-1. **Social Security and Medicare Contribution Rates for Workers and Employers, Selected Years, 1940–90**

Year	Annual maximum taxable earnings (dollars)	Contribution rate (percent of taxable earnings)					
		Employers and employees, each			Self-employed		
		OASDI[a]	HI[b]	Total	OASDI[a]	HI[b]	Total
1940	3,000	1.00	. . .	1.00	. . .	. . .	. . .
1945	3,000	1.00	. . .	1.00	. . .	. . .	. . .
1950	3,000	1.50	. . .	1.50	. . .	. . .	. . .
1955	4,200	2.00	. . .	2.00	3.00	. . .	3.00
1960	4,800	3.00	. . .	3.00	4.50	. . .	4.50
1965	4,800	3.62	. . .	3.62	5.40	. . .	5.40
1970	7,800	4.20	0.60	4.80	6.30	0.60	6.90
1975	14,100	4.95	0.90	5.85	7.00	0.90	7.90
1980	25,900	5.08	1.05	6.13	7.05	1.05	8.10
1985	39,600	5.70	1.35	7.05	11.40	2.70	14.10[c]
1990	48,600[d]	6.20	1.45	7.65	12.40	2.90	15.30[c]

Sources: *Background Material and Data on Programs within the Jurisdiction of the Committee on Ways and Means: 1986 Edition,* Committee Print WMPC 99-14, 99 Cong. 2 sess. (Government Printing Office, 1986), pp. 67 and 69; and *1988 Annual Report of the Board of Trustees of the Federal Old-Age and Survivors Insurance and Disability Insurance [OASDI] Trust Funds* (Baltimore, Md.: Social Security Administration, 1988), tables D3 and E1, pp. 126–27.
   a. Old-age, survivors, and disability insurance.
   b. Hospital insurance.
   c. In 1985, an income tax credit of 2.3 percent was given, so the net contribution rate paid was just 11.8 percent. In 1990, one-half of OASDHI contributions can be claimed as a deductible business expense; hence, the net contribution rate is generally less than 15.3 percent.
   d. Projected under alternative II-B assumptions.

under past and current law on employers, employees, and the self-employed and the maximum earnings subject to taxation. This maximum is increased each year in proportion to growth in economywide average earnings, excluding earnings of the self-employed.

Revenues from payroll taxes greatly exceeded initial old-age and survivors benefits until the mid-1950s (table 2-2). Despite the initial buildup in the trust fund, interest earnings on social security reserves were relatively unimportant because the program was so small. From 1955 through 1985 social security was essentially financed on a pay-as-you-go basis, with income from payroll taxes more or less covering annual benefit payments.

Pay-as-you-go financing of social security benefits permitted Congress to keep payroll tax rates low during the early years of the program, because few people had yet qualified for benefits while most workers were making payroll tax contributions. As the number of beneficiaries and per capita benefits increased, the tax rate was gradually raised.

TABLE 2-2. Income, Expenditures, and Reserves of the Social Security Trust Funds, Selected Years, 1940–90

Millions of dollars

Year	Income				Expenditures			Net increase in trust funds	Trust fund reserve at end of year
	Net contributions	From taxation of benefits	Net interest	Total[a]	Benefit payments	Total[b]			
1940	325	...	43	368	35	62		306	2,031
1945	1,285	...	134	1,420	274	304		1,116	7,121
1950	2,667	...	257	2,928	961	1,022		1,905	13,721
1955	5,713	...	454	6,167	4,968	5,079		1,087	21,663
1960	11,876	...	569	12,445	11,245	11,798		647	22,613
1965	17,205	...	651	17,857	18,311	19,187		-1,331	19,841
1970	34,737	...	1,791	36,993	31,884	33,108		3,886	38,068
1975	64,259	...	2,866	67,640	67,022	69,184		-1,544	44,342
1980	116,711	...	2,330	119,712	120,598	123,550		-3,838	26,453
1985	194,149[c]	3,430	2,741	203,540	186,075	190,628		11,088	42,163
1990[d]	288,486[c]	4,669	16,257	309,527	246,374	252,209		57,318	211,932

Source: *1988 OASDI Annual Report,* tables 19 and 23, pp. 56 and 64.
a. Includes payments from the general fund of the Treasury not shown separately.
b. Includes administrative expenses, transfers to the Railroad Retirement program, and interfund borrowing transfers to and from the hospital insurance trust fund.
c. Includes federal government contributions on deemed credits for military service.
d. Projected under alternative II-B assumptions.

One side effect of this procedure—and one reason for the enormous initial popularity of social security—was that early retirees received benefits vastly in excess of their tax contributions. Even workers who are now retiring or who will retire within the next couple of decades can expect to receive benefits that provide unsustainably high rates of return on the tax contributions that they and their employers have made.[7] During most of their work lives, current retirees faced tax rates well below those necessary to pay fully for the benefits they will get.

Low tax rates are no longer feasible. The tax rate required to finance a mature pay-as-you-go program depends on the replacement rate offered by the program, the rate of growth of average wages, and the ratio of beneficiaries to the number of workers currently making payroll tax contributions. The higher the replacement rate, the slower the rate of growth of wages, and the larger the ratio of beneficiaries to active workers, the higher the tax rate that is required. The number of OASDI beneficiaries per one hundred covered workers rose from two in 1945 to twenty in 1960 and to thirty in 1985 (figure 2-1). The growing proportion of retirees in the population and the lengthening average life span mean that an increased share of current wage earnings must be set aside to finance pensions for those over sixty-five.

For three decades after World War II, the increase in payroll tax rates was slowed by the rapid growth of the work force, especially after 1960. This growth meant that for each new retiree several young workers were starting employment. If the size of the work force had instead remained stable, the ratio of retirees to workers would have risen much faster. The projected future increase in the ratio of beneficiaries to active workers is significant and is responsible for much of the widespread concern that the cost of social security will become a major burden on active workers in the future.

A second trend holding down payroll tax rates was the rapid rise in average earnings, which reflected high productivity growth before 1973. Since pensions of retirees are based on their past earnings, while revenues depend on the size of the current wage base, the

7. For a historical review and projection of individual social security benefits relative to contributions, see Robert J. Myers and Bruce D. Schobel, "A Money's-Worth Analysis of Social Security Retirement Benefits," *Transactions of the Society of Actuaries*, vol. 35 (1983), pp. 533–45 and 555–61.

FIGURE 2-1. **Ratio of Beneficiaries to Covered Workers in Social Security Program, Selected Years, 1945–85**

Beneficiaries per 100 covered workers[a]

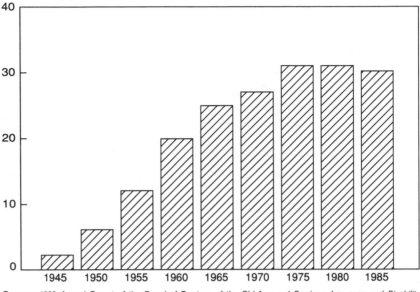

Source: *1988 Annual Report of the Board of Trustees of the Old-Age and Survivors Insurance and Disability Insurance Trust Funds* (Baltimore, Md.: Social Security Administration, 1988), table 30, p. 79.
a. Beneficiaries include retired and disabled workers, spouses, children, and survivors.

faster earnings rise, the larger is the taxable wage base in relation to the total cost of retirement benefits.[8]

In 1977 and 1983, Congress cut benefits and increased taxes. The effect was to generate large surpluses starting in the 1980s that could be used later to help meet high pension costs expected in the twenty-first century. As a result social security surpluses will for the first time become significant. Table 1-3 shows the importance of these surpluses in the short run, and chapter 3 describes how their economic significance will grow in subsequent decades.

Trust Fund Investments

Any excess of OASDHI income over current expenses is placed in separate OASI, DI, and HI trust funds as reserves. These reserves by

8. For example, if real wages rise 20 percent in each decade, a pension equal to 40 percent of the final wage of retiring workers will equal only 33 percent of the average wage of workers ten years later. On the other hand, if real wages fail to grow, the pension will continue to represent 40 percent of the average economywide wage throughout the worker's entire retirement.

TABLE 2-3. **Number of Beneficiaries and Total Benefits Payments under Social Security and Medicare, Selected Years, 1940–87**

Year	Beneficiaries (thousands)				Benefit payments (percent of GNP)		
	OAI[a]	SI[b]	DI[c]	HI[d]	OASDI	HI	SMI[e]
1940	148	74	...	...	0.03	...	...
1945	691	597	...	...	0.14	...	...
1950	2,326	1,152	...	...	0.35	...	...
1955	5,788	2,172	...	...	1.23	...	...
1960	10,599	3,558	687	...	2.18	...	...
1965	14,175	4,953	1,739	...	2.60	...	...
1970	17,096	6,468	2,665	20,361	3.14	0.50	0.19
1975	20,364	7,368	4,352	24,640	4.19	0.71	0.27
1980	23,336	7,601	4,678	28,067	4.41	0.92	0.39
1985	25,991	7,160	3,907	30,109	4.64	1.19	0.57
1987	26,970	7,157	4,045	31,400[f]	4.55	1.10	0.69

Sources: *Social Security Bulletin*, vol. 51 (January 1988), pp. 21–22; *Background Material: 1987 Edition*, pp. 88 and 139; *Social Security Bulletin, Annual Statistical Supplement, 1982* (Baltimore, Md.: Social Security Administration, 1982), p. 204; *1988 Annual Report of the Board of Trustees of the Federal Hospital Insurance Trust Fund* (U.S. Department of Health and Human Services, Health Care Financing Administration, 1988), table 6, p. 36; and *1988 Annual Report of the Board of Trustees of the Federal Supplementary Medical Insurance Trust Fund* (Health Care Financing Administration, 1988), table 6, p. 26; and *1988 OASDI Annual Report*, tables 23, A2, and A3, pp. 64, 100, and 104.
  a. Old-age insurance.
  b. Survivors insurance.
  c. Disability insurance.
  d. Hospital insurance. Number of people insured, not number receiving payments.
  e. Supplementary medical insurance.
  f. Projected.

law must be invested in securities guaranteed as to principal and interest by the federal government. Nearly all trust fund assets are held in special public-debt obligations issued by the Treasury and available only for purchase by the trust funds. The Social Security Act mandates that these securities when issued bear an interest rate approximately equal to the average market yield on all outstanding government securities that are not due or callable for at least four years. A small share of trust fund assets has occasionally been invested in federally sponsored agency obligations. (Social security investment policy is examined in chapter 6.)

Beneficiaries and Cost

From modest beginnings, both the number of beneficiaries and the cost of social security benefits have grown enormously (table 2-3). The number of beneficiaries grew rapidly during the 1940s and 1950s because of the sharp rise in the fraction of workers reaching sixty-five who had become insured under the program. Benefit outlays also rose because of increases in average earnings of new pensioners and because of the legislated increases in benefits. Since 1960 the rate of growth in the number of old-age and survivor beneficiaries and in the level of benefits has slowed. Growth rates are expected to slow still further in the immediate future because of a small decline in the number of Americans reaching retirement age. Spending on disability insurance, after rising sharply through the mid-1970s, has grown at a moderate pace over the past decade. Changes in future DI outlays will depend largely on trends in wages and changes in the legal and administrative definition of disability.

Medicare outlays have followed a different pattern. The 1965 social security amendments granted full and immediate eligibility for HI and SMI benefits to most elderly Americans. The growth in medicare spending has been rapid, not only because the number of beneficiaries has increased, but also because the use and cost of medical services have risen. Measured in constant dollars, medicare expenditures more than tripled in the eleven years after 1973, rising more than 11 percent a year. Medicare enrollment grew by a little less than one-quarter that rate.

Real spending on medicare benefits has proven harder than pension benefits to predict accurately. Accumulated pension entitlements depend on past average earnings, which at each moment depend heavily on partly completed wage histories and on the number of beneficiaries. Both of these variables can be predicted with little error, at least over the next couple of decades. In contrast, outlays on medicare depend not only on the size of the insured population, but also on hard-to-forecast variables such as the real cost of medical care and the fraction of the insured population that receives care.

The Social Security Benefit Formula

Cash benefits for workers and their survivors or dependents are based on the worker's employment record in jobs covered by social security. Workers who have accumulated enough earnings credits in covered employment and who meet certain other conditions can currently receive full pensions at sixty-five, the normal retirement age under the program, and can receive actuarially reduced benefits as early as age sixty-two. Insured workers who become disabled are eligible for disability insurance cash benefits if they are unable to engage in any substantial gainful activity by reason of a physical or mental impairment that is expected to last at least a year. Social security benefits are not subject to any means test.[9]

Until 1984 OASDI benefits were exempt from federal income taxation. Beginning in 1984, up to one-half of OASDI benefits has been counted in taxable income.[10] The proceeds of this tax, which are deposited in the OASI and DI trust funds, now provide about 1.5 percent of annual trust fund income. The importance of revenue from this tax will increase because the thresholds above which benefits are taxed have not been indexed. As time passes, therefore, the real thresholds will fall and an increasing proportion of benefits will become subject to tax.

A worker's exact monthly pension depends on many factors, including the worker's age when benefits begin, number of eligible family members, and current earnings. The starting point for all benefit calculations, however, is the insured worker's average monthly earnings in covered employment.

Although the exact benefit formula has been changed often, the formula has remained explicitly redistributive (table 2-4). Workers with low average earnings receive higher benefits in relation to their past earnings than do workers with high average earnings. Since all workers face the same payroll tax rate, poorly paid workers enjoy a higher rate of return than do well-paid workers on their tax contributions.[11]

Another constant has been the periodic adjustment in the level of benefits for new beneficiaries to assure that pensions do not fall sharply in relation to a worker's pay just before retirement. In fact, as the figures in table 2-4 show, the replacement rate actually rose

9. However, beneficiaries under seventy years old are subject to an earnings test. Disability insurance benefits are stopped if the beneficiary earns more than $300 a month (except during periods of "trial work"), and OASI benefits are reduced if the beneficiary's annual earnings exceed specified thresholds.

10. Taxpayers whose adjusted gross incomes plus one-half of social security benefits plus tax-free interest incomes exceed certain limits ($25,000 for single taxpayers and $32,000 for married couples filing joint returns) must pay taxes on up to one-half of their social security benefits.

11. The explicit redistribution inherent in the benefit formula is partly offset by the greater longevity of highly paid workers, who typically survive to collect old-age pensions for more years than low-wage pensioners. On the other hand, low-wage workers are more likely than are high-wage workers to receive disability benefits and, because of higher mortality rates, to generate benefits for young survivors.

TABLE 2-4. **Old-Age Insurance Replacement Rates for Retirement at Age Sixty-five, by Earning Level, Selected Years, 1950–2040**

Percent of previous year's earnings[a]

Year	Low earner[b]	Average earner[b]	High earner[b]
1950	44.7	30.0	26.8
1955	49.6	34.6	32.8
1960	45.0	33.3	29.8
1965	40.0	31.4	32.9
1970	42.7	34.3	29.2
1975	59.5	42.3	30.1
1980	64.0	51.1	32.5
1985	63.8	40.9	22.8
1990	69.7	42.3	24.7
2000	66.5	41.3	25.6
2010	59.1	38.5	25.4
2020	56.1	38.1	25.6
2030	51.0	35.8	24.1
2040	51.0	35.8	24.1

Sources: *Background Material: 1987 Edition*, p. 93; Sylvester J. Schieber, *Social Security: Perspectives on Preserving the System* (Washington, D.C.: Employee Benefit Research Institute, 1982), p. 26, for 1950 rates; and *Social Security Bulletin, Annual Statistical Supplement, 1987*, p. 14.

a. For single workers becoming entitled in January at age sixty-five, the sum of twelve monthly benefit payments divided by earnings in year prior to entitlement. Rates in 2010 and later years adjusted to reflect the rise in normal retirement age scheduled under the 1983 social security amendments.

b. For the average earner, annual earnings in each year of the work career are assumed to be equal to average earnings in the economy. The low earner is assumed to receive earnings approximately one-half those of the average earner, and the high earner to earn the taxable maximum earnings throughout his career.

during the late 1960s and most of the 1970s as basic benefits were liberalized.[12]

The computation of benefits depends on the primary insurance amount (PIA), which is the pension for a single retired worker who begins to receive old-age benefits at the normal retirement age (currently sixty-five). Virtually all other OASDI benefits are set equal to some percentage of the PIA. The PIA for any particular worker is based on the worker's average indexed monthly earnings (AIME) in employment covered by social security. For workers turning sixty-two after 1990, the computation will be based on the worker's earnings in the thirty-five years of highest covered earnings up to age sixty-two or his age when he applies for benefits, whichever occurs later. The Social Security Administration multiplies wages in each year of the earnings record by an index factor that reflects the growth in

12. The projected drop in replacement rates after 2001 reflects the gradual increase in the age at which unreduced benefits can be received, from sixty-five to sixty-seven. Thus, aged sixty-five retirees, who now receive full retirement benefits, will receive actuarially reduced benefits starting in 2003.

economywide wages since that year. For example, if average wages when a worker was thirty are one-half of those when the worker turns sixty, the worker's taxable wages earned at age thirty would be doubled for the calculation of average monthly earnings. (Wages earned at or after age sixty are not indexed in this way, however.)

The PIA is simply a percentage of the worker's average earnings. In 1988 this percentage was

90 percent of the first $319 in AIME plus

32 percent of the AIME above $319 but less than $1,922 plus

15 percent of any AIME above $1,922.[13]

The dollar amounts in this formula—the bend points—are adjusted each year to reflect the growth in economywide average wages. The formula is clearly redistributive, because workers with low average wages obviously receive pensions that are a higher percentage of past wages than workers with monthly incomes above $319.

The indexation of wages earned before age sixty and the annual adjustment of the bend points in the PIA formula ensure that average benefits rise at the same rate as average wages. Initial benefits increase in real terms if wages grow faster than prices and fall if prices grow faster than wages. Once the PIA is computed (using the formula in effect when the worker reaches age sixty-two), it is adjusted thereafter for increases in prices, not wages. This procedure assures that the purchasing power of benefits remains constant for those with no current earnings.

One feature of the basic pension formula is particularly important in the results of this study. The formula establishes a close link between the average real retirement benefit paid to a particular cohort and the economywide real wage when the cohort reaches age sixty. The exact benefit formula for that cohort depends on the economywide average wage level when the cohort turns sixty, not on that cohort's wage history over its entire working life. If economywide wages rise by 10 percent in the year that a birth cohort turns age sixty, the average indexed earnings of that cohort will be increased 10 percent— and its average benefit level will be raised 10 percent as well— although the payroll taxes of this cohort will rise only in the year during which the jump in wages occurs. In this way, the social security formula links initial pension levels to wage levels just before retire-

13. *Social Security Bulletin*, vol. 51 (January 1988), p. 2. For insured workers under sixty-two who become disabled or die in 1988, the same PIA formula is also used, with earnings indexed to calendar year 1986 rather than to age sixty.

ment. The connection between pensions and lifetime tax contributions is much more tenuous.

Economic Effects

Social security and medicare play an important part in shaping fiscal policy of the federal government. They also have played a major part in determining the economic status of individual workers and beneficiaries.

Trust Fund Operations

Treatment of operations of the social security and medicare trust funds in the federal budget has not been consistent over time. Until 1969 the income and outlays of the trust funds were not included in the "administrative" budget of the federal government, the budget total on which most public attention and congressional debate focused.[14] Thus, any surplus or deficit in the trust funds had no effect on the most commonly reported government surplus or deficit.

After 1969 OASI, DI, and HI revenues and expenditures were included in the "unified" budget, and any difference between OASDHI payroll tax revenues and outlays was fully reflected in the current federal budget deficit or surplus. Note that interest earnings of the trust funds did not affect the unified federal budget because the interest was paid by other parts of the government that were also included in the unified budget. In addition, interest was recorded on a "net" basis—expenses minus receipts—on the expenditure side of the budget. Hence, within the unified budget, interest income of the social security and medicare trust funds was exactly offset by interest outlays of other government departments.

Following the recommendations of the 1982 National Commission on Social Security Reform, Congress in 1983 removed OASDI and HI (but not SMI) operations from the unified federal budget, but delayed the effective date of removal until 1993. Under a provision of the Gramm-Rudman-Hollings Balanced Budget Act in 1985, OASDI operations were technically designated an off-budget item in the federal budget.[15] Another provision of the 1985 act short-circuits this poten-

14. The trust funds were part of the "consolidated cash" budget and the "national income and products account" budget, which drew much less attention than the administrative budget.

15. Operations of the HI trust fund are still not scheduled to move off the unified budget until 1993, however.

tially significant change by requiring that OASDI operations be included in deficit-reduction targets. Thus, effectively, the OASDI program remains in the unified federal budget.

How accountants treat social security and medicare is less important than how the trust funds affect fiscal policy. When tax receipts for social security and hospital insurance exceed outlays, the trust funds purchase U.S. Treasury securities. These purchases reduce federal borrowing from private lenders and free private saving for private investments, in the United States or abroad. If the trust funds run deficits, they are forced to sell some of their securities back to the Treasury to raise cash to make benefit payments. Thus, trust fund surpluses directly increase government saving, and trust fund deficits reduce government saving. That is not true, however, if the balance on other government accounts is modified to offset trust fund operations.

Well-being of the Elderly

The OASDI program has been conspicuously successful in raising the income of elderly and disabled Americans. Social security benefits account for about 60 percent of the cash income received by poor families with an aged family member. They constitute over one-quarter of the income received by nonpoor families with an aged family member and an even larger percentage for older people who live alone.[16] The steady increase in benefits has reduced the percentage of elderly and disabled Americans living in poverty. In 1959, when 22.4 percent of the general population had incomes below the official poverty threshold, over 35 percent of those over sixty-four years old were poor. By 1985, when the poverty rate for all Americans had fallen to 14.0 percent, the rate for older Americans had fallen to just 12.6 percent—1.4 points below the rate for the general population. If the value of in-kind benefits such as housing assistance and medicare were taken into account, the poverty rate among the elderly would represent an even lower fraction of poverty among the general population.[17] In fact, the average income and consumption of the

16. *Background Material and Data on Programs within the Jurisdiction of the Committee on Ways and Means: 1986 Edition,* Committee Print WMPC 99-14, 99 Cong. 2 sess. (GPO, 1986), pp. 82, 84.

17. For example, in 1986 the poverty rate among the elderly was 91 percent of the rate among the general population when only cash forms of income are counted. Including noncash forms of income, the relative rate among the elderly is even lower.

aged are now comparable to those of the rest of the population, even though some elderly groups, such as aged widows, continue to suffer from high poverty rates.

That this progress is due in large part to social security is suggested by the fact that other important sources of income among the aged—especially wage earnings—have fallen dramatically in recent decades. In 1960, for example, a third of all men over the age of sixty-four were in the labor force; by 1985, the rate of participation for that group had fallen to 16 percent. Among aged women, the participation rate fell from 11 percent to 7 percent over the same period. Rising social security benefits have more than offset the decline in earnings as the elderly have moved out of the labor force.

The recent gains of the elderly have not been based solely on social security and medicare benefits, of course. The number of beneficiaries under private pension plans has grown explosively in recent decades, rising from 1.8 million in 1960 to 9.1 million by 1980.[18] Pension plans in 1985 provided incomes to nearly four of every ten household units with a member aged sixty-five or older and provided about 13 percent of the cash incomes received by these household units.[19]

Income from retirement savings is another growing source of support for families with aged members. In 1962 slightly more than half of elderly couples and single people received asset income, and this income provided 16 percent of their annual incomes. By 1985 the proportion receiving this kind of income rose to two-thirds, and asset income comprised more than one-quarter of annual family income. In all, the share of elderly family income arising from social security, public and private pensions, and asset income has risen from 56 percent to nearly 80 percent since 1962.[20] The dependence of the elderly on wage earnings and financial contributions from younger relatives is gradually disappearing.

Even though retirement income from private sources has risen in recent decades, there is little doubt that social security and medicare

---

This generalization is true for all of the alternative definitions of poverty used by the Census Bureau, including definitions that exclude noncash medical benefits.

18. Alicia H. Munnell, *The Economics of Private Pensions* (Brookings, 1982), p. 11.

19. By comparison, social security and Railroad Retirement pensions were received by 93 percent of older household units (counting both families and unrelated individuals) and provided 32 percent of their incomes. *Background Material: 1987 Edition*, p. 112.

20. *Social Security Bulletin*, vol. 50 (May 1987), p. 7.

benefits have made a vital contribution to improving the economic status of the elderly, especially the elderly living in low-income families. Social security payments are the principal source of cash income for the majority of aged Americans, and medicare covers about half of their medical bills.[21]

Ironically, the very success of social security and medicare in raising the incomes of the elderly has inspired sharp criticism of the programs. The elderly now enjoy living standards roughly equal to those of the rest of the population and experience poverty rates well below those of American children. Under these circumstances, many critics of programs for the aged see little justification for the continued growth in spending. This perception may grow sharper over the next several decades if these programs impose rising tax burdens on the working-age population.

21. *Economic Report of the President, 1985,* p. 174; *Background Material: 1988 Edition,* p. 177.

CHAPTER 3

Outlook for the Programs

SINCE 1941 Congress has required the trustees of social security to report annually on projected outlays and revenues. Because social security promises to pay benefits many years into the future, the social security actuaries prepare three sets of projections, looking five, twenty-five, and seventy-five years into the future. Until recently, the longest projection period for health insurance (HI) was just twenty-five years, reflecting the great uncertainty concerning future hospital costs and rates of utilization. For the past few years, however, the annual report of the HI trustees has also contained long-term projections for the program covering the next seventy-five years.

Like other financial organizations, the social security and medicare programs must satisfy two conditions—liquidity and solvency. The programs are liquid if at each point in time the sum of current revenues and accumulated revenues is sufficient to cover all expenses. They are solvent if, over the long run, total revenues equal or exceed total obligations. For both social security and medicare the long run is seventy-five years.[1]

The Actuaries' Long-Range Projections

In assessing the financial status of the trust funds, the actuaries use two principal measures. The first, known as the contingency fund ratio, indicates the liquidity of the system. This measure is the ratio of trust fund reserves at the beginning of each year to anticipated expenditures in that year.[2] If the contingency fund ratio in a particular year were 50 percent, for example, the trust fund reserve would be large enough to pay about six months' outgo.

At the beginning of 1988 the fund ratio for old-age, survivors, and disability insurance (OASDI) was 41 percent. Under the intermediate

1. Before 1965 the long-term actuarial projections looked at the balance of the system in perpetuity. *Report of the National Commission on Social Security Reform* (GPO, 1983), app. J, p. 5.
2. The trust fund is credited with the amount of transfers from the Treasury paid in anticipation of payroll tax receipts covering the month of January.

34

assumptions used in the 1988 report of the OASDI trustees, it was expected to rise above 500 percent in the second decade of the next century and fall thereafter.[3] A contingency reserve of 8 percent to 9 percent of annual outgo is needed if the fund is to make timely benefit payments because of the mismatch between the flow of revenues and expenditures. The contingency fund ratio of the hospital insurance program was slightly above 100 percent at the beginning of 1988; it was expected to rise until the 1990s and then begin to fall.[4]

The second financial measure—the actuarial balance of the fund—is based on a comparison of the cost rate and the income rate of the programs over the next seventy-five years. The income rate in a particular future year is defined as the combined rate of employees' and employers' contributions scheduled for that year, plus the projected rate of income from taxation of benefits expressed as a percentage of taxable payroll.[5] The cost rate for a given year is the outgo for benefits and administrative expenses, expressed as a percentage of taxable earnings. For the entire projection period, the actuarial balance is the difference between the income rate and the cost rate, each measured over the next seventy-five years. The OASDI programs are considered to be in close actuarial balance if the income rate is within 5 percent of the cost rate. If the income rate were less than 95 percent of the cost rate—falling short of close actuarial balance—Congress would be expected either to cut benefits or to raise revenues enough to bring the gap within a 5 percent range. Congress has shown far less concern about the long-term solvency of the HI program, requiring only that the program's short-term position be secure.

The OASDI and HI actuaries use somewhat different methods to summarize annual income and cost rates over their medium- and long-term projection periods. The procedure used in the HI program—and in the OASDI program before 1988—is to calculate the average income rate of the program as the arithmetic average of annual income rates over the seventy-five years of the projection. Similarly, the

3. *1988 Annual Report of the Board of Trustees of the Federal Old-Age and Survivors Insurance and Disability Insurance [OASDI] Trust Funds* (Baltimore, Md.: Social Security Administration, 1988), pp. 4–7.

4. *1988 Annual Report of the Board of Trustees of the Federal Hospital Insurance [HI] Trust Fund* (Washington, D.C.: U.S. Department of Health and Human Services, Health Care Financing Administration, 1988), p. 5.

5. Taxable payroll is wage and self-employment earnings that are subject to OASDI or HI payroll taxes. Note that the income rate does not include interest income earned on the trust fund reserves.

average cost rate is calculated as the arithmetic average of annual cost rates over the same period. The actuarial balance of the HI program is measured by determining the ratio of the average income rate to the average cost rate.

The OASDI actuaries in 1988 adopted a level financing method for determining actuarial balance. They calculate the present value of future income, outgo, and taxable payroll, discounting future annual amounts at the assumed future rate of interest. Income and cost rates over the projection period are obtained by dividing the present values of tax income and outgo, respectively, by the present value of taxable payroll. The income rate is then adjusted to reflect the initial trust fund balance. The trust fund is expressed as a percentage of taxable payroll in the first year of the projection and then added to the income rate for the succeeding seventy-five years. If the adjusted income rate is within 5 percent of the cost rate, the OASDI trust fund is said to be in close actuarial balance.[6]

Of course, the long-term projections prepared by the OASDI and HI actuaries depend sensitively on a variety of economic and demographic assumptions. Like astrologers and futurologists, economists have limited success predicting events one year in the future, much less seven decades later. The value of the economic projections lies not in their capacity to accurately foretell the future, but in their representation of the logical implications of carefully stated economic and demographic assumptions.

Demographic Assumptions

The long-range projections rest on detailed assumptions about beneficiary populations, average benefit rates, and taxable payroll. In estimating the number of future beneficiaries and taxable workers, the actuaries rely on three sets of demographic assumptions, yielding

---

6. The OASDI valuation procedure is preferable to the one used by the HI actuary. First, the OASDI level financing method properly gives credit for current reserves held in the trust fund; the HI procedure essentially ignores these reserves. The difference is not significant when trust fund reserves are low, as they were in the late 1970s and early 1980s. It becomes increasingly important, however, when the trust fund represents several years' benefit outlays, a position the OASDI fund is expected to achieve by 2010. Also, the level financing method implicitly gives proper credit for interest income earned by the trust fund. The HI procedure only does so if the future interest rate coincides with the assumed rate of growth in taxable earnings.

an optimistic, an intermediate, and a pessimistic projection. Optimistic assumptions are those associated with a large revenue base and a small flow of benefits, a combination that permits relatively low tax rates. Pessimistic assumptions, in contrast, lead to projections of a small revenue base and relatively high benefits.

The critical assumptions used by the actuaries to project future benefits and taxes vary from year to year, as new information becomes available and interpretations of historical information change. The descriptions in this chapter are based on assumptions and projections contained in the 1988 report of the OASDI trustees, the first report that used level financing as a basis of calculation. Our simulation results in later chapters rely on detailed assumptions and projections that served as a basis for the 1986 reports of the OASDI and HI trustees.[7]

The optimistic demographic projection used in the OASDI trustees' 1988 report is based on an assumption that the total fertility rate will reach 2.2 children per woman by the year 2011. Under the intermediate and pessimistic projections, the total fertility rates are assumed to stabilize at 1.9 children and 1.6 children per woman, respectively. In fact, birth rates have been running a little below those assumed in the intermediate projection—they reached a low of 1.74 in 1976 and then rebounded somewhat to 1.81 in 1979 and rose to 1.87 in 1987.[8] The rate assumed in the intermediate projections in 1988 thus approximates recent experience.[9]

The fertility assumptions are combined with assumptions regarding future mortality and immigration to derive projections of the age composition of the population. Falling mortality rates are good news for each person individually, but the faster they fall the higher are the taxes active workers will have to pay to support pension and health benefits for the retired and disabled. Increased immigration affects the cost of social security much like increases in birth or

7. *Economic Projections for OASDHI Cost and Income Estimates, 1986,* Actuarial Study 98 (Baltimore, Md.: Social Security Administration, 1987). Detailed projections are generally not available until several months after publication of the relevant annual report; those for 1986 were the most recent available when this book was written.

8. U.S. Bureau of the Census, *Statistical Abstract of the United States, 1988* (GPO, 1987), p. 59. Under current mortality conditions and with no immigration, a total fertility rate of 2.11 would eventually produce a stable population.

9. Under the intermediate demographic assumptions of the 1986 report, used in the simulations in chapter 4 below, the total fertility rate was projected to stabilize at 2.0 children per woman.

FIGURE 3-1. **Ratio of Beneficiaries to Covered Workers in Social Security Program under Three Demographic Assumptions, 1970–2060**

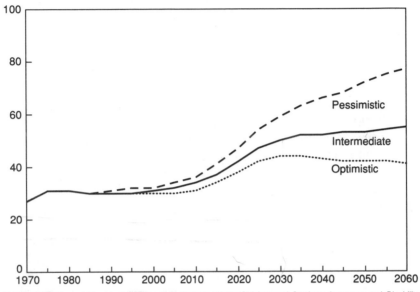

Beneficiaries per 100 covered workers[a]

Source: *1988 Annual Report of the Board of Trustees of the Old-Age and Survivors Insurance and Disability Insurance Trust Funds* (Baltimore, Md.: Social Security Administration, 1988), table 30, pp. 79–80.
   a. Beneficiaries include retired and disabled workers, spouses, children, and survivors.

mortality rates—it increases the ratio of workers to retirees. The optimistic, intermediate, and pessimistic assumptions about mortality and immigration define a range within which the actuaries believe U.S. experience is likely to fall over the next seventy-five years.

The ratio of OASDI beneficiaries to covered workers rose over most of the postwar period. It has now reached a plateau, as figure 3-1 shows, that under the optimistic, intermediate, and pessimistic assumptions used in 1988 will last until 2010, when the baby-boom generation begins to retire. The OASDI dependency ratio will then climb rapidly and gradually stabilize once again around 2035, except under pessimistic demographic assumptions. As these projections indicate, the ratio is highly sensitive to events, such as future birth, immigration, and death rates, that no one knows how to forecast very precisely. But under all three projections, the number of beneficiaries to be supported by each active worker is slated to rise quite sharply early in the next century.

Economic Assumptions

Projections of social security benefits and revenues rest on economic as well as demographic assumptions. The most critical economic variables are the rate of growth of real wages and the real interest rate.[10]

In 1988 the OASDI actuaries' optimistic projection was based on the assumption that labor productivity would ultimately grow 2.3 percent a year, beginning early in the next century. This is an extremely high rate compared with the 0.9 percent annual productivity increase observed in the decade after 1977. The pessimistic projection assumed that productivity growth would stabilize at 1.5 percent a year after 2010. The actuaries also report two sets of intermediate economic assumptions, one based on the premise that labor productivity will grow at 1.7 percent and the other on the premise that productivity will rise 2.0 percent each year after 2010. The more pessimistic of these two assumptions combined with the intermediate demographic assumptions results in the II-B projection, which is used as a standard in most public discussions of social security.[11] In all cases, productivity growth is assumed to accelerate between 1988 and 2010. Each of the long-run productivity assumptions appears optimistic in light of recent experience. Even the 1.5 percent rate assumed in the pessimistic projection is well above the rate the United States has experienced since the oil crisis of 1973. (The effect of lowering the assumed rate of productivity growth is examined in chapter 4.)

Real hourly compensation would generally be expected to rise as fast as worker productivity. Two factors break this link. First, workers in the future may receive a changed percentage of their pay in the form of taxable money wages. The proportion of compensation paid in the form of untaxed fringe benefits, such as medical insurance

10. Contrary to common view, the rate of inflation has only a small long-run effect on projections of social security balance. Even more surprising, increased inflation slightly reduces long-term social security costs assuming that higher inflation affects wages and consumer prices equally. The gain arises because a rise in both prices and wages increases revenues immediately but boosts outlays only after a lag. The net long-term effect is small. If unexpected inflation affects consumer prices without affecting nominal wages, the consequences for social security are obviously different; the long-term solvency of the program would be harmed.

11. Under the II-B assumptions used in the 1986 report, the projected rate of productivity growth after 2010 is 2.1 percent (see *OASDHI Economic Projections, 1986*, pp. 1–19 and 44). The 1986 projection is 0.4 percent a year faster than the assumed rate in the *1988 OASDI Annual Report*, p. 95.

premiums and pension contributions, has been rising. Under the most optimistic projection the actuaries assume that this trend will proceed at a slower pace in the future than it has in the recent past, and under the most pessimistic projection that it will accelerate. Under the intermediate projection that combines the intermediate demographic assumption and the more pessimistic of the two intermediate sets of economic assumptions (the II-B projection), the 1988 report projects that fringe benefits will rise from about 17 percent of compensation in 1987 to 29 percent of compensation seventy-five years later, in 2062.[12]

Taxable wages are also likely to grow more slowly than productivity because the average work week is shrinking. Over the three decades following 1950, average paid hours per week fell 11 percent.[13] Under the intermediate II-B projection used in the 1988 report, the average work week is assumed to fall about 1.5 percent each decade, to about thirty-four and one-half hours per week by 2062.[14] Obviously it is very difficult to predict fringe benefits and the length of the work week very far into the future, but the current intermediate projections appear reasonable.

Before 1988 the interest rate played no direct role in the OASDI actuaries' long-term assessment of financial solvency, because long-term costs and benefits were simple averages of each year's average costs and tax revenues. This omission mattered little when social security was financed on a pay-as-you-go basis and projected interest earnings on the trust funds were negligible. When trust funds become large, however, interest earnings will rise correspondingly, and it is important to take account of the real interest rate in projecting long-term revenues, as the OASDI actuaries have done for the 1988 report.

Under current law and the II-B projections used in 1988, the combined OASDI trust funds will grow until 2031 and remain positive until 2048.[15] These reserves, which are invested in Treasury debt

12. The fringe benefit assumptions in the 1988 annual report are the same as those used in *OASDHI Economic Projections, 1987*, p. 80. Under the II-B assumptions in *OASDHI Economic Projections, 1986*, p. 113, fringe benefits were projected to rise even faster, to 34 percent of compensation by 2060.

13. *OASDHI Economic Projections, 1986*, p. 100.

14. Private communication from the Office of the Actuary, Social Security Administration. In *OASDHI Economic Projections, 1986*, p. 98, the actuaries projected a much faster decline in the average work week—about 3 percent per decade.

15. *1988 OASDI Annual Report*, p. 142, and discussion with Stephen Goss in the Office of the Actuary.

instruments, earn a real rate of return that is ultimately determined by interest rates in the financial market. With large trust fund reserves, the total income—including interest income—earned by the funds will be sensitive to even modest changes in the real rate of return. Higher rates of return would add to the trust fund reserves, while lower rates would reduce them. Real interest rates under the four economic projections range from 1.5 percent under the most pessimistic assumption to 3 percent under the most optimistic. The assumed rate under the II-B projection is 2 percent after 1998.[16] Unlike the assumptions regarding productivity, the assumed real interest rate may be somewhat pessimistic, as real interest rates in recent years have considerably exceeded 2 percent. Should real interest rates remain above 2 percent, the actuaries are likely to consider increasing the rate used in their intermediate projection. (The implications of a real interest rate of 3 percent are discussed in chapter 4.)

The actuaries' detailed projections of future economic and demographic trends are not intended to represent exact predictions of the future state of the economy or the social security and medicare trust funds. They are designed instead to provide "indicators of the trend and range of future [trust fund] income and outgo, under a variety of plausible economic and demographic conditions."[17] While no one projection prepared by the actuaries can be accepted as the single best forecast of future trends, the president and Congress generally rely on the II-B projections to guide them in establishing future tax rates. In this volume the II-B assumptions contained in the trustees' 1986 report are used to examine the effects of alternative social security financing policies. Appendix A summarizes some significant changes introduced in the 1987 and 1988 reports.

Social Security Balance: Past and Future

Figure 3-2 depicts the future financial status of social security under the 1986 II-B demographic and economic assumptions (the II-B assumptions for 1987 and 1988 imply an almost identical pattern of income and outlays). Projected tax receipts, benefit payments, taxes plus interest receipts, and OASDI trust fund reserves are measured as percentages of contemporaneous net national product (that is, gross national product less depreciation of the capital stock). For about

16. *1988 OASDI Annual Report*, pp. 34–35.
17. Ibid., p. 33.

FIGURE 3-2. **Income, Expenditures, and Reserves of the**
Social Security Trust Funds, 1986–2060

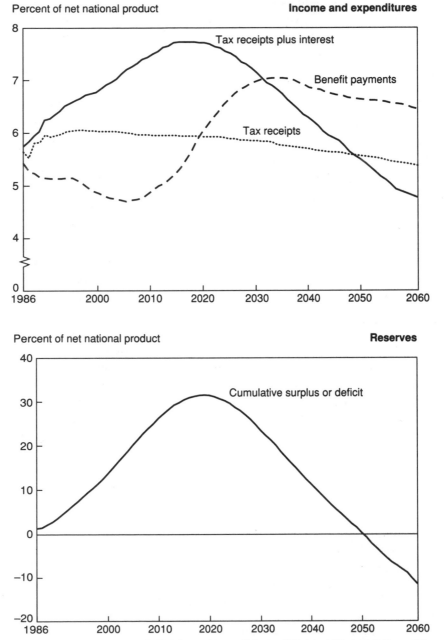

Percent of net national product   **Income and expenditures**

Sources: *Economic Projections for OASDHI Cost and Income Estimates, 1986,* Actuarial Study 98 (Baltimore, Md.:
Social Security Administration, 1987); SSA, Office of Actuary, unpublished data; and authors' calculations.

fifteen years outlays fall as a share of net national product and for several decades remain well below revenues. With the rapid growth of reserves, interest on the trust funds becomes a major source of revenue, rising to 20 percent of total receipts by 2010. After 2020, however, the growing proportion of retirees in the population will raise benefit payments above tax revenues. Just after 2030, outlays will begin to exceed the sum of tax receipts and interest income on the trust funds. By 2045, the yearly gap between taxes and benefits will exceed 1 percent of net national product and the trust funds will be exhausted around 2050. Under the II-B assumptions in the 1986 OASDI trustees' report, social security will then accumulate liabilities that will equal about 11 percent of net national product by 2060.[18]

Although the combined trust funds for old-age, survivors, and disability insurance are projected to be exhausted around 2050 under the intermediate II-B assumptions, the social security system is nonetheless regarded as solvent over its long-term planning horizon, since revenues projected over the next seventy-five years are within 5 percent of costs over the period. In 1986, using the average cost method of valuation, projected outlays under the II-B assumptions equaled 13.40 percent of taxable earnings. Revenues were projected to be 12.96 percent of taxable payroll, or about 97 percent of OASDI tax revenues. Under the level financing method and intermediate assumptions used in the 1988 report, costs were projected to be 13.52 percent of taxable payroll, while projected revenues were 12.94 percent of payroll or 96 percent of costs. The combined OASDI trust funds were therefore considered to be in close actuarial balance in both the 1986 and the 1988 reports.

Close actuarial balance can be achieved with a large short-term surplus, as under current law; or with a small contingency reserve, as under strict pay-as-you-go financing; or with even larger reserves than those scheduled under current law. Though all of these alternatives could achieve close actuarial balance, they would generate very different patterns of trust fund accumulation (whose economic effects are explored in chapters 4 and 5).

Twice during the 1970s and early 1980s the liquidity or solvency of the OASDI trust funds was in jeopardy. In the mid-1970s, the

18. Under the optimistic projection, reserves are expected to grow continuously over the next seventy-five years, while under the pessimistic projection, costs will substantially exceed revenues over the period and reserves will be exhausted around 2025. Ibid., p. 83; and *1986 OASDI Annual Report*, p. 75.

formula for computing initial pension payments provided unintentionally excessive adjustments for inflation, threatening the solvency of the system. Although the problem was corrected in 1977 before it could undermine liquidity, a long-term imbalance between revenues and benefit obligations remained.

The failure of real wages to grow as rapidly as anticipated in the late 1970s and early 1980s further undermined solvency and threatened the short-term liquidity of the system. Solvency deteriorated because revenues projected at the reduced rates of growth of real earnings could not sustain promised benefits for seventy-five years. Liquidity of the system was jeopardized because the trust funds, already depleted by revenue shortfalls traceable to slow growth of real earnings, were in danger of falling too low to cover monthly benefit payments. [19]

The liquidity problem, which affected only the old-age and survivors insurance trust fund, was resolved by special legislation that allowed the fund to borrow reserves from the disability and hospital insurance trust funds. The solvency problem exposed by the II-B projections was corrected by the social security amendments of 1983, which delayed promised cost-of-living increases, speeded up previously scheduled payroll tax increases on employees and employers, gradually increased the normal retirement age for those reaching age sixty-five after 2002, returned to the trust funds the proceeds of a new income tax on a part of social security benefits, and boosted the contribution rate of the self-employed.

The Threat to Close Actuarial Balance

The possibility that social security will experience liquidity problems any time soon seems remote. The question of solvency, however, is virtually certain to recur within a few years. The II-B projections will sooner or later move into deficit because revenues exceed outlays in the first part of the projection period and fall short in the latter part. Each successive annual long-term projection will contain one fewer early year with a large surplus and one additional later year with a large deficit. For example, the projection period in the 1986 report

19. Before passage of the 1983 social security amendments, reserves had to be approximately 15 percent of anticipated annual benefit payments. If they fell below that level, the trust funds had to obtain bridge financing from another trust fund or the U.S. Treasury.

included 1986, a year with a surplus equal to 0.50 percent of taxable payroll. The 1987 report excluded 1986 but included 2061, a year with a deficit of 2.74 percent of payroll. Although the effects of moving forward one year are small, they cumulate and must eventually push the II-B projection out of close actuarial balance. Each year this development increases the deficit (or lowers the surplus) by 0.03 to 0.05 percent of taxable payroll.[20]

When social security is out of close actuarial balance, Congress customarily restores balance by either raising taxes or cutting benefits. Some time in the not-too-distant future Congress will be obliged to make this choice or modify the concept of close actuarial balance. In one sense, then, the current projections might be viewed as internally inconsistent.

To better reflect the probable financial status of the trust funds over the next seventy-five years, we estimated two new tax schedules using the II-B demographic and economic assumptions in the 1986 report, but with the additional assumption that future Congresses will maintain close actuarial balance in the OASDI program in each year of the planning horizon. Actuarial balance will be maintained by periodically adjusting the payroll tax rate while continuing to meet benefit commitments implied by the currently scheduled benefit formula.[21]

One way to maintain balance, of course, is to fund social security benefits under a strict pay-as-you-go tax formula. This policy would require that OASDI revenues just equal outlays each year, plus a small additional amount to maintain reserves equal to, say, six months or one year of outlays. Pay-as-you-go tax rates would closely resemble the cost rates projected under the II-B assumptions. Interest income on the funds would remain negligible.

Another way to maintain close actuarial balance is to accumulate a trust fund considerably larger than necessary merely for contingencies,

20. Deficits would not emerge if an increase in immigration, birth rates, labor-force participation, growth of productivity, or personal income tax rates tended to increase revenues or a fall in the disability rate or a rise in mortality tended to reduce benefit costs.

21. The assumption that the tax rate will be raised, while the benefit formula will be left unchanged, is clearly arbitrary, but it is computationally a simpler adjustment to perform than those entailing changes in benefits. The alternative extreme assumption is that benefits will be trimmed by exactly enough to maintain close actuarial balance, holding constant the current schedule of future tax rates.

or, in other words, to partially fund future benefit obligations. Congress implicitly adopted this strategy when it adopted the 1977 and 1983 social security amendments.

We computed the future tax rates Congress would impose assuming it wished to leave future benefit levels unchanged while keeping the OASDI program in close actuarial balance. To calculate actuarial balance, we used a discounting procedure that is essentially the same as the level cost methodology adopted by the OASDI trustees in their 1988 report.[22]

Our definition of close actuarial balance requires that the present value of social security resources—including the initial trust fund reserves—remain within 5 percent of the present value of future program costs. The present value of resources is the sum of the initial trust fund balance and the values of projected future tax collections discounted over the seventy-five-year planning horizon at the rate of return on the trust funds assumed under the II-B projection. Similarly, the present value of future costs is the sum of discounted future OASDI outlays over the projection period. If the present value of resources falls below 95 percent of discounted costs, the payroll tax must be raised enough to restore equality between the present values of social security resources and program costs.

The detailed projections in the 1986 OASDI trustees' report provide too little information for analysis of years beyond 1986. To measure the long-term solvency of the program in 2001, for example, requires detailed projections of taxable payroll and benefits for the seventy-five years from 2001 through 2075, the last fifteen of which are not covered in the 1986 report. To derive estimates for each year not covered in the 1986 report, we used the actuaries' II-B assumptions to project taxable wages and benefits through 2135.[23]

If Congress decides to raise taxes when the long-term projection indicates that outlays exceed revenues by more than 5 percent, it must still decide how promptly to implement the tax increase. In our calculations, the tax change is assumed to take effect the year after social security resources fall below 95 percent of discounted social security costs. Actuarial balance is restored by a flat increase in the payroll tax rate over the entire seventy-five-year projection period.

22. Our calculations were performed before the OASDI trustees adopted the level cost methodology, so the discounting procedures may differ slightly.

23. Our projections for the years 2061 through 2100 closely match unpublished projections for those years prepared by the OASDI actuaries' office.

FIGURE 3-3. **Social Security Payroll Tax Rates under Current Law,
Pay-as-You-Go Financing, and a Periodically Adjusted Level
Tax Schedule, 1986–2060**

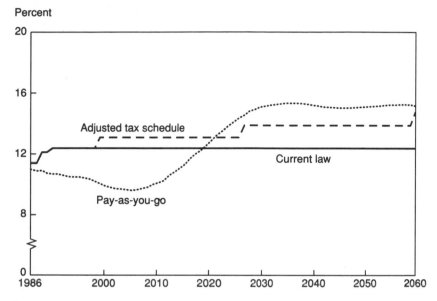

Sources: *1986 OASDI Annual Report*, p. 12; and SSA, Office of the Actuary, unpublished data in support of *1986 OASDI Annual Report*.

Throughout this volume we refer to the resulting tax schedule as the periodically adjusted level tax schedule. Admittedly, this policy may not be the most realistic one from a political perspective or the most desirable one on equity grounds. But it is a useful one to examine because it shifts a larger share of the burden of future retirement costs from future to current workers.[24]

Figure 3-3 shows the payroll tax rates required to keep social security in close actuarial balance over the next seventy-five years under pay-as-you-go financing and under a policy of partially funding future social security benefits with the periodically adjusted level tax. The figure also shows the combined employee-employer OASDI tax schedule under current law, which calls for the rate to reach 12.4

24. If long-term deficits appear in a year when current revenues exceed current outlays, Congress might postpone the tax increase. The later the increase takes effect within the seventy-five-year planning horizon, however, the larger it must be. We examined the consequences of delaying the scheduled tax increase for twenty years after the year in which social security resources fall below 95 percent of discounted costs; the delay had little effect on our main conclusions.

percent in 1990 and remain at that level thereafter. If OASDI had been funded on a pay-as-you-go basis in 1986, the payroll tax rate would have been only about 11 percent and would decline further to 9.7 percent by 2005; it would then rise to 15.1 percent in 2030, by which year most of the baby-boom generation will have retired. Under a strict pay-as-you-go system, the children and grandchildren of the baby-boom generation would therefore face tax rates more than half again above those faced by the baby-boom generation itself.

Under the currently legislated tax schedule, the social security system will slip out of close actuarial balance in 1999. If Congress raises payroll taxes in that year to restore close actuarial balance over the following seventy-five-year period, a tax increase in 1999 of slightly more than 0.7 percentage point would be required. Subsequent tax increases of 0.8 percent would be required in both 2027 and 2060. The tax rate would thus reach 14.7 percent by 2060. Except for the final year of the projection period, the tax rate would not exceed 13.9 percent, considerably below the 15.1 percent rate required under a pay-as-you-go formula and only modestly higher than the currently legislated rate of 12.4 percent.

Figure 3-4 shows the accumulation of social security reserves as a percentage of net national product under the tax schedule contained in current law and under our periodically adjusted level tax schedule. Under current law a large trust fund will be accumulated, reaching a maximum of 32 percent of net national product in 2019. This trust fund then falls and is exhausted by about 2050. Under the alternative tax schedule, the accumulation of reserves is larger, the decline in the trust fund measured as a fraction of net national product is more modest (in real dollars, it does not fall), and the trust fund is never depleted.

The Outlook Including Medicare

While old-age, survivors, and disability insurance was adequately financed (that is, in close actuarial balance) in 1988 under current assumptions and estimating procedures, the hospital insurance program was deeply in deficit. Official projections published in 1988 suggested that hospital insurance faces deficits of 0.43 percent, 2.64 percent, and 4.03 percent of taxable earnings in the next three twenty-five-year periods. The average deficit over the next seventy-five years

FIGURE 3-4. **Social Security Trust Funds as a Percentage of Net National Product under Current Law and a Periodically Adjusted Level Tax Schedule, 1986–2060**

Percent

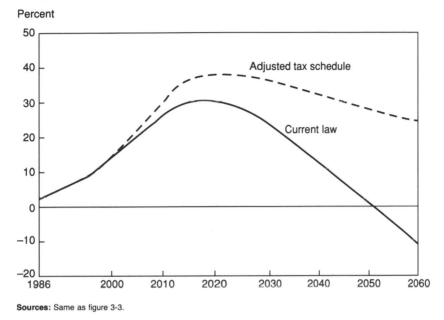

Sources: Same as figure 3-3.

is 2.37 percent of taxable payroll.[25] Furthermore, the reserves of the hospital insurance system were projected to be exhausted by 2005.[26] The large projected deficits in the HI fund will eventually force Congress either to increase revenues of the HI system or to cut benefits unless the rate of growth of hospital spending falls precipitously.

The future deficits in the HI fund are large in part because medicare will eventually face the same sharp increase in the number of beneficiaries as the OASDI system. In addition, however, the cost of hospital care per beneficiary is projected to rise much faster than the growth of taxable earnings. If these costs rose at the same rate as

25. These statistics refer to the "augmented balance" projections; *1988 HI Annual Report*, p. 47. The long-term deficit projections are more optimistic than those contained in *1986 HI Annual Report*, p. 46, which showed a seventy-five-year average deficit equal to 3.02 percent of taxable payroll.

26. *1988 HI Annual Report*, p. 10. The projected date of trust fund depletion under the II-B assumptions was 1996 in *1986 HI Annual Report*, p. 9.

general price inflation, the long-term deficit in the HI trust fund would be far smaller.[27]

Because future HI deficits are so large, major tax increases will be necessary to keep both OASDI and HI in close actuarial balance. Substantial combined surpluses in OASDI and HI over the next two to three decades will be followed by large and growing deficits. According to the II-B projections prepared in 1988, the combined surplus over the twenty-five years through 2012 amounts to 1.72 percent of taxable payroll. But in the next two twenty-five-year periods the combined deficits will be 4.09 percent and 7.35 percent of payroll, respectively. During the latter period, this deficit is projected to be nearly one-third of combined OASDI and HI outlays.[28]

The HI deficit could be closed with either a strict pay-as-you-go tax schedule or a tax schedule that keeps HI in close actuarial balance over each succeeding projection period. Figure 3-5 shows the combined OASDI and HI tax rates under current law as well as the rates necessary under pay-as-you-go financing and our alternative periodically adjusted level tax for the period 1986–2060.[29] Figure 3-6 shows

27. From 1974 to 1985 the number of people insured under hospital insurance rose by 29 percent. If hospitalization payments had risen 118 percent, which was the rate of general price inflation as measured by the consumer price index, overall HI spending would have gone up about 177 percent. In fact, HI payments were up slightly more than 400 percent, *1987 HI Annual Report*, p. 71. Hospitalization payments rose more than prices in general because hospital utilization rose and hospital price inflation greatly exceeded growth in other prices.

28. *1988 OASDI Annual Report*, p. 72; and *1988 HI Annual Report*, p. 47. Both the deficit and the cost rate are calculated using the average cost valuation method, so interest earnings of the trust funds are ignored. Because the HI outlook has improved since 1986, the combined OASDI and HI long-term position is somewhat better according to the 1988 report than the 1986 report. Simulations in this volume are based on the 1986 projections.

29. The HI payroll tax rates required under a pay-as-you-go system closely mirror the cost rates reported in the *1986 HI Annual Report*. The periodically adjusted level tax rates required under the partially funded system were computed to keep the HI program in close actuarial balance over a twenty-five-year horizon, rather than the seventy-five-year horizon used for OASDI. Until 1988, a twenty-five-year horizon was customarily used to assess the solvency of the HI system. Long-range forecasts for hospital insurance are notoriously unreliable because the formidable uncertainties associated with demographic and economic projections are compounded in the case of medicare by the virtual impossibility of anticipating the nature and cost implications of scientific discoveries affecting medical care. Our choice of projection horizons also seems consistent with the way Congress and the president view solvency in the HI program as compared with OASDI.

FIGURE 3-5. **Combined Social Security and Hospital Insurance Payroll Tax Rates under Current Law, Pay-as-You-Go Financing, and a Periodically Adjusted Level Tax Schedule, 1986–2060**

Percent

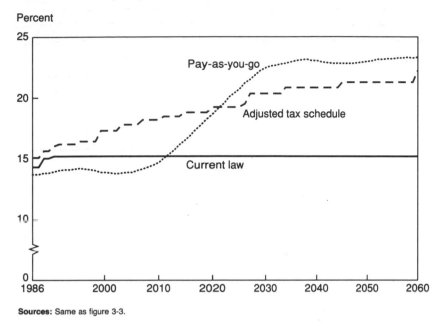

Sources: Same as figure 3-3.

the size of the combined OASDI and HI trust funds under current law and the periodically adjusted level tax schedule.

Unlike figure 3-3, which shows the required OASDI tax rates alone, figure 3-5 indicates that major tax increases will be needed to maintain the solvency of social security and medicare. By the end of the projection period in 2060, the required tax is 22.2 percent—nearly half again as large as the currently scheduled payroll tax rate. This increase reflects not only aging of the population but also spiraling medical care costs. If these costs could be contained, the aging of America would appear far less costly to future workers.

Summary

The United States is one of a handful of countries that publish official long-range projections of the costs and revenues of major social insurance programs. These projections make possible an informed debate about whether the costs imposed by these programs are ones

FIGURE 3-6. **Combined Social Security and Hospital Insurance Trust Funds as a Percentage of Net National Product under Current Law and a Periodically Adjusted Level Tax Schedule, 1986–2060**

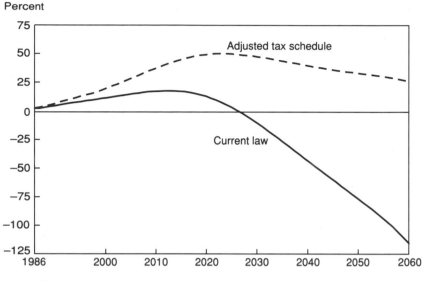

Sources: Same as figure 3-3.

the electorate wishes to bear. In most respects, the assumptions underlying the OASDI projections are defensible. But the assumptions regarding future growth of productivity seem to be unduly optimistic, and those regarding future real interest rates too pessimistic. Unless labor productivity rebounds or real interest rates fall, the assumptions underlying the long-run projections must gradually be modified. The social security actuaries ordinarily change their assumptions as information becomes available or trends persist. For example, the assumed fertility rates have been gradually reduced as actual fertility rates have remained low; in 1988 the assumed fertility rate almost exactly matched actual fertility in 1987.

One could quarrel endlessly about specific aspects of the projections, because there is little basis for making reliable projections over such a lengthy time horizon. Consider, for instance, how actuaries working for President Woodrow Wilson would have anticipated labor productivity, medical costs, and fertility rates of the late 1980s in evaluating public policies in 1915.

For our purpose, however, the projected future levels of variables under the II-B assumptions provide a convenient baseline for mea-

FIGURE 3-7. **Social Security and Hospital Insurance Outlays as a Share of Net National Product, 1986–2060**

Percent of net national product

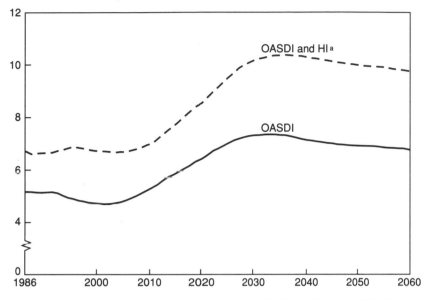

Sources: *OASDHI Economic Projections, 1986*, pp. 113 and 122; SSA, Office of Actuary, unpublished data; and authors' calculations.
a. Old-age, survivors, and disability insurance and hospital insurance.

suring the effects of alternative government policies. We concentrate on the differential effects of changes in the national saving rate. The precise path of the baseline projection is not critical to our conclusions. Furthermore, the actuaries' projections under a variety of different economic and demographic assumptions do reveal an underlying pattern that is common to all but the most optimistic projections. Under the current schedule of payroll tax rates, the social security accounts will be in surplus through the first third of the next century and will face large and growing deficits thereafter. The hospital insurance program will experience more modest surpluses in the next several years and massive deficits starting early in the next century. From the point of view of the main trust fund accounts, the future is clearly divided into alternating periods of feast and famine.

The growth and then the collapse of the trust funds is attributable in part to the huge shift in the age composition of the population that will occur over the next three decades. Figure 3-7 shows the trend in projected OASDI and HI outlays as a percentage of net national product. The sharp rise in spending beginning in 2010 coincides with the onset of retirement among the oldest cohort of baby-boom workers. Outlays on OASDI benefits and administrative expenses rise more than 10 percent between 2010 and 2030, from under 5 percent of NNP to over 6 percent. Over the same twenty-year interval, spending on hospital insurance is projected to grow by about half, rising from 2 percent of NNP to 3 percent of NNP. The combined burden of the OASDI and HI programs on the economy will rise nearly by half, from 7.1 percent of NNP in 2010 to 10.2 percent in 2030.

In spite of the projected growth in outlays, the OASDI and HI payroll tax rates are scheduled under current law to remain constant after 1990, leading to the eventual depletion of trust fund reserves. We believe this aspect of the long-term projections is misleading. The assumption that taxes can remain unchanged over a long period when underlying costs are rising strongly is untenable. Current projection methods obscure the inevitability of change, either in benefits or in tax rates.

To remedy this deficiency, we have calculated the payroll tax rates that will be needed to keep the trust funds in actuarial balance each year over the next seventy-five years. These tax rates provide a more realistic picture of tax burdens facing future workers if the current benefit schedule is to be maintained. Under these alternative rates, the trust funds will continue to grow, even after the baby-boom generation has begun to retire. Instead of feast and famine, the trust funds would experience feast followed by an indefinite period of comparative plenty.

CHAPTER 4

An Economic Model for Analyzing Social Security

THE PROJECTIONS used in the annual reports of the social security trustees are based, in part, on the assumption that many of the economic determinants will follow historical trends. The trustees explore the sensitivity of their projections by estimating the effects of variations in some of the basic assumptions. Our interest is less in testing the specific assumptions than in forecasting the consequences of changes in current policies—especially in alternative uses of the projected surplus. Our analysis requires an explicit economic model that clearly specifies the links among assumptions about demographic trends, technical change, and economic growth. The model must provide a consistent framework for evaluating the effects of changes in either the assumptions or policy.

Our model of economic growth projects the future burden of social security and medicare benefits and shows the consequences of alternative methods of paying for those benefits. This chapter summarizes the model and uses it to examine how an increase in national saving affects the growth of the economy, the social security system, and the burdens of social security benefits on future generations. By changing some of the basic economic assumptions underlying our model or used by the social security actuaries, we can project the future status of the old-age, survivors, and disability insurance (OASDI) trust funds. The next chapter uses the model to measure the economic consequences of various methods of paying for the future costs of social security and medicare.

A Model of Economic Growth

This chapter focuses on the OASDI program and its interaction with the remainder of the U.S. economy. Our model of U.S. economic growth is calibrated so that our baseline projection duplicates exactly the path of employment, real output, wages, and social security revenues, outlays, and reserves in the alternative II-B projections used in the OASDI trustees' report for 1986.[1]

The model goes beyond those projections, however. It contains additional detail on private and government saving and investment and shows the links among changes in the capital stock, output, and the rate of return to capital in the private sector.[2] The model traces out the process by which increases in national saving add to the stock of capital, future output, and wage income, and lower rates of interest. Because social security benefits and revenues depend on wage earnings, changes in saving will also affect the financial status of the social security system.

Thus, the model can be used to explore the effects on the economy as a whole, and on social security in particular, of changes in government budget policies. The full model, including more than one hundred equations, is discussed in appendix B. The model emphasizes long-term growth and ignores the business cycle.

The Private Economy

We assume that the projections of labor supply (labor hours) under the intermediate, II-B assumptions will hold in the future; thus we make no independent effort to project population, labor force participation, unemployment, and average hours of work per year.[3] The critical elements of our model involve the determination of national saving, its allocation between domestic and foreign investment, and the process by which changes in the rate of capital accumulation affect the growth of output and incomes in future years.

We used a basic saving-investment identity to equate investment with private saving plus government saving, the latter consisting of the surplus or deficit in the social insurance accounts and the surplus

1. *1986 Annual Report of the Board of Trustees of the Federal Old-Age and Survivors Insurance and Disability Insurance [OASDI] Trust Funds* (Baltimore, Md.: Social Security Administration, 1986). Use of projections for 1988 would not have affected our results materially.

2. The projections of the social security actuaries do not incorporate explicit assumptions about saving and investment rates. Instead, they project directly the rate of growth of output per labor hour in line with historical trends. To differentiate between gains in productivity that result from improved technology and the influence of increased capital formation, we developed an explicit representation of saving, investment, and the relationship between capital and output.

3. *Economic Projections for OASDHI Cost and Income Estimates, 1986*, Actuarial Study 98 (Baltimore, Md.: Social Security Administration, 1987), pp. 2–15.

or deficit for the rest of government.[4] On the investment side, total national saving is divided between domestic investment in housing and business plant and equipment and net foreign investment.

In our initial baseline projection we assume that the fraction of gross national product saved privately will equal the postwar average of 18 percent (including pension funds of state and local governments). This regularity in private saving has been christened Denison's Law after the economist who first noted the absence during most of this century of any trend in the proportion of GNP saved by U.S. households and businesses.[5] To make our projections consistent with postwar historical averages, we assume that government dissaving—the budget deficit—will fall from 3.7 percent of gross national product in 1987 to 1.5 percent by 1992 and remain constant as a share of GNP thereafter.

Domestic investment is just the difference between total national saving (private plus public) and net foreign investment. We consider two extreme possibilities about net foreign investment. In one we set net foreign investment equal to zero, a condition that means that all fluctuations in national saving are reflected in domestic investment. This assumption implies that the United States never runs a current account surplus or deficit with the rest of the world and that no net capital movements occur in or out of the the United States regardless of relative rates of return in different countries. In the baseline case, after a transition lasting from 1986 through 1992, national saving and gross domestic investment are both a constant 16.5 percent share of GNP.

In reality, financial capital can move internationally in response to changes in relative rates of return in the United States and abroad. These capital flows do give rise to movements of real resources, which are expressed as net surpluses or deficits in the balance of trade in goods and services. To examine the effects of such movements, we assume alternatively that domestic U.S. investment is determined

4. We include the surplus or deficit of state and local governments in the category of "rest of government," but add the pension fund reserve of state and local employees to private saving to parallel treatment of private sector pensions, which are part of household saving in the national income and product accounts. As a result the state and local fiscal balance is always close to zero.

5. See Edward F. Denison, "A Note on Private Saving," *Review of Economics and Statistics*, vol. 40 (August 1958), pp. 261–67. For an examination of the historical data, see Paul A. David and John L. Scadding, "Private Savings: Ultrarationality, Aggregation, and 'Denison's Law,' " *Journal of Political Economy*, vol. 82, pt. 1 (March–April 1974), pp. 225–49.

independently of domestic saving. This assumption means that all variations in U.S. saving show up as changes in net foreign investment (the implications of foreign investment are considered in chapter 5).

We project output and employment in four sectors—agriculture, government, nonprofit institutions, and private households—on the basis of historical trends. The U.S. national accounts do not include changes in labor productivity in these sectors, except in agriculture, where changes in productivity are dominated by technological changes. We project those changes in line with historical trends so that output and employment in the four sectors remain the same in all of our simulations.

Output in the nonfarm business sector, however, is obtained from a production function that relates output to the available stock of capital, labor hours, and the rate of technological progress.[6] The capital stock is calculated as the cumulative sum of past business investment less depreciation. Thus, changes in investment gradually influence output through their effect on the stock of capital. Each 10 percent increase in the capital stock increases output by 3 percent. Increases in the capital stock also change wage rates and the return to capital, or profits. A higher ratio of capital to labor leads to a proportionate increase in real wage rates and a decline in the profit rate. We assume that the rate of technical change is independent of the rate of change in capital and labor—disembodied technical change. Thus, in contrast to the view that high rates of investment speed up the introduction of new technology, our model minimizes the influence of capital on output.[7]

In the baseline projections we adjusted the assumed rate of technical change (total factor productivity growth) so that the model produces in each year the same GNP as assumed in the social security actuaries' 1986 II-B projections.[8] The implied rate of technical progress required to match the II-B projections appears to be unreasonably rapid when compared with recent trends. Between 1950 and 1973 the rate of technical progress averaged about 15 percent per decade, but in the decade ending in 1985 it slowed to less than 6 percent. The II-B projections imply that over the next seventy-five years technical change will average no less than 12 percent per decade, and sometimes

6. We assume a Cobb-Douglas production function. See appendix B.
7. On the issue of embodied technical change, see Robert M. Solow, "Growth Theory and After," *American Economic Review*, vol. 78 (June 1988), pp. 307–17.
8. *OASDHI Economic Projections, 1986*, p. 108, table 19c.

as much as 16 percent *per decade*. In other words, the social security actuaries' intermediate economic assumptions in 1986 implied a recovery of total factor productivity growth to a rate that is high by historical standards.[9] The trustees' 1988 projections use somewhat lower assumed rates of growth in productivity than did the 1986 report; yet they include offsetting changes in other areas that would cause our substantive conclusions to be much the same as under the 1986 projections.[10] We examine some of the implications of changing the baseline economic assumptions in the last section of this chapter.

The social security actuaries assumed that the real interest rate earned on government securities (alternative II-B) will decline sharply from 7.6 percent in 1985 to 2 percent by 1996 and remain constant thereafter.[11] This assumption is defensible, but it is difficult to reconcile with our other baseline assumptions. If investment as a share of GNP remains near the historical average, and if the growth of the labor supply slows, as suggested by the demographic projections, the ratio of capital to output will rise strongly over the next seventy-five years. A rising capital-output ratio would normally be associated with a steady decline in the rate of return on physical capital throughout the whole period. If, as generally assumed, the real rate of interest on financial assets bears some relation to the return on physical capital, the real interest rate would also decline over most of the seventy-five-year projection period, not just over the first ten years.

To resolve this discrepancy, we adopt a conversion ratio between the return on physical and financial capital sufficient, in the baseline simulation, to produce the II-B projection of the financial interest rate. This procedure allows deviations from the baseline in the real after-tax rate of return on physical capital to lead to proportional deviations from the baseline in the real interest rate on financial

9. The high rate of growth of productivity in the nonfarm business sector is not obvious when reading the actuaries' reported projections of economywide increases in labor productivity. In 1986 the actuaries assumed that, for the entire economy, labor productivity growth would recover from its current low rate, but that it would never fully return to the robust rates of the 1950s and 1960s. Those past high rates, however, reflected both technical efficiency gains within individual sectors and reallocations of labor from farming to higher productivity sectors (nonfarm). The shift of labor between these sectors contributed 0.3 percentage point per year to economywide productivity growth between 1948 and 1986, but this type of reallocation has slowed. Future gains in economywide productivity growth will depend far more than in the past on increases in total factor productivity within the nonfarm business sector.

10. See appendix A.

11. *OASDHI Economic Projections, 1986,* p. 68, table 12c.

assets. In effect, we compute the rate of return on capital required to maintain private investment demand at a level consistent with full employment, and then assume that monetary policy will be changed to allow a corresponding adjustment of the rate of return on financial assets.

Finally, the rate of inflation is determined outside the model and equals 4 percent annually in the years after 1990, as assumed by the II-B projections.[12] Thus, we add the rate of inflation to the real interest rate and to the change in real wage rate to obtain nominal values. The rate of inflation has very little effect on the long-run position of the social security fund because both revenues and benefits are indexed for inflation.

Social Security

To develop a detailed representation of social security revenues and outlays, we calibrated revenues, disbursements, and reserves in the baseline simulation to match the II-B projections of the social security actuaries. Annual revenues consist of payroll taxes, federal income taxes imposed on benefits, and interest on the previous trust fund balance. Annual expenditures are simply equal to the average benefit payment times the number of beneficiaries, plus administrative costs. Thus, the annual surplus or deficit is defined as tax revenues plus interest receipts less expenditures. The tax rates are those specified in the II-B projections and the number of beneficiaries is held at the level projected by the social security actuaries. The model determines the tax base, the average benefit payment, the interest rate, and the fund balance. The tax base is proportionate to the economywide wage bill, because the taxable wage ceiling is automatically adjusted for increases in the average nominal wage rate.

On the benefit side, we distinguish between new and existing retirees. The initial benefit received by a retiree is a fraction of the worker's past average wages which depend in turn on economic conditions. Increases in the average aggregate real wage lead to proportionate increases in the average real benefit paid to new retirees.[13] Thus, the average real new benefit is simply a weighted

12. Ibid., p. 49, table 9b.
13. The formula for the average benefit payable to recipients of disability insurance is similar. The benefit paid to survivors or dependents is a fraction of the basic benefit paid to primary disabled or retired beneficiaries or a fraction of what would have been paid to decedents.

average of past economywide wage rates. Benefit payments to existing retirees are adjusted each year for price inflation as measured by the consumer price index. Finally, the trust fund balance at the end of the year is equal to the prior year's balance plus the current year's surplus.

The Benefits of Increased Saving: An Illustration

The easiest way to examine the operation of the model is by examining the economic consequences of an increase in national saving. To illustrate such an increase, we changed the assumption about the future budget deficit, reducing it by 1.5 percent of GNP in each year of the simulation period. Thus the budget is balanced in 1992 and thereafter, and the change increases each year's national saving by 1.5 percent of gross national product. We assume that this addition to saving does not prevent the achievement of full employment. In effect, we assume that adjustments in monetary policy are sufficient to maintain the same employment path as in the baseline II-B case. In addition, we continue to assume that the saving is all invested domestically.

Effects on the Economy

The major economic effects of increased saving are summarized in table 4-1 as percentage deviations from the baseline case. The higher rate of national saving is fully reflected in a higher domestic rate of capital accumulation. The capital stock expands gradually until it reaches a new level, 15.3 percent above its baseline value (column 1). Eventually, the increased depreciation just offsets the extra gross saving, and the capital stock ceases to expand relative to the baseline path. The enlarged stock of capital eventually raises net national product (NNP) by 3.0 percent (column 2). The percentage gain in output is far less than the increase in the capital stock because, with a fixed labor supply, each 1.0 percent increase in the capital stock increases gross output by just 0.3 percent. Column 3 shows the effect on private consumption.

Part of the additional national income shows up as increased real wages, which rise by 4.7 percent at the end of the projection period (column 4). However, with a higher ratio of capital to output, the rate of return to physical capital declines—a diminishing marginal return. Thus, market interest rates must also decline in line with the

TABLE 4-1. **Economic Impact of a Permanent Rise in Saving Achieved by Reducing Government Deficits from 1.5 Percent to 0.0 Percent of Gross National Product, Selected Years, 1990–2060**

Year	General economy (percent change from baseline)					Social security trust fund (percent change from baseline)				Incremental burden (percent of NNP)[a]	
	Capital stock (1)	Net national product (2)	Consumption[b] (3)	Wage rate (4)	Nominal interest rate[c] (5)	Payroll taxes (6)	Benefits (7)	Interest receipts[d] (8)	Trust fund reserve[e] (9)	Baseline (10)	Higher saving (11)
1990	0.0	0.0	0.0	0.0	0.0	0.0	0.0	0.0	0.0	0.0	0.0
2000	7.0	1.4	-0.2	2.3	-0.09	2.3	0.3	0.4	0.6	-0.4	-0.2
2010	11.3	2.2	0.9	3.6	-0.28	3.6	1.7	0.3	1.6	-0.3	-1.1
2020	13.3	2.5	1.4	4.2	-0.38	4.2	3.0	-0.7	1.7	1.0	-0.2
2030	14.3	2.7	1.7	4.4	-0.44	4.4	3.7	-1.5	0.9	1.8	0.5
2040	14.9	2.9	1.8	4.6	-0.46	4.6	4.1	-1.5	-0.1	1.6	0.2
2050	15.1	2.9	1.9	4.6	-0.47	4.6	4.4	-1.1	-0.6	1.4	-0.1
2060	15.3	3.0	2.0	4.7	-0.47	4.7	4.5	-0.2	-0.7	1.2	-0.3

Source: Authors' calculations as explained in the text.

a. The increase in the ratio of old-age, survivors, and disability insurance (OASDI) benefits to baseline net national product (NNP) from the 1986–90 average, minus the increase in consumption from the baseline level, expressed as a percent of NNP in the baseline.

b. Private consumption plus all government expenditures (includes government investment-type outlays).

c. Expressed as the simple difference from the baseline in percentage points.

d. Expressed as a percent of total OASDI income.

e. Expressed as a percent of NNP in the baseline.

lower return on physical capital if incentives to expand investment are to be maintained (column 5). Overall, both labor and capital income rise, the first because of increased wages per worker, and the second because there is more capital, albeit with a slightly lower return per unit.[14]

Effects on Social Security

The increase in economywide earnings causes payroll tax revenues to rise contemporaneously and proportionately to the change in earnings (column 6). Average social security benefits are also increased, although with a lag. By the end of the projection period, benefits have increased 4.5 percent (column 7), nearly matching the rise in the real wage rate.

It might seem that the OASDI trust funds would benefit from an increase in saving, because revenues rise before outlays. However, as a repository of financial assets, the trust funds also suffer losses from the reduced rate of return in financial markets (column 8).[15] In addition, since outlays slightly exceed revenues over the full seventy-five years in the baseline case, a proportionate increase in each causes the difference between them—the deficit—to rise.

On balance, the long-run financial condition of social security is not improved by an increase in government saving, even one that is permanent. In fact, an increase in saving slightly raises the share of OASDI benefits in national income and reduces the level of trust fund reserves after 2030. This occurs because the baseline II-B projections show benefits exceeding taxes for the seventy-five-year projection period as a whole, and the model itself ultimately produces equal percentage increases in taxes and benefits.

While an increase in saving may not benefit the social security trust funds, it generates large benefits for all future generations, even after they have paid the greater cost of a higher level of benefits. For example, the increase in saving eventually boosts net national product by 3.0 percent but raises social security benefits by only 0.3 percent of net national product.

14. The percentage increase in wages exceeds that of NNP because the latter excludes capital consumption allowances (depreciation). These allowances rise in proportion to the rise in the capital stock. In addition, wage rates are tied to productivity in the business sector where the percentage gain in output is larger than that for the economy as a whole.

15. The change in interest receipts is expressed as a percent of total baseline revenues because interest income is negative in the last few years of the projection.

TABLE 4-2. **Derivation of Incremental Burden under Higher Saving Alternative Shown in Table 4-1**

| Year | Ratio of OASDI benefits to NNP (percent) (1) | Baseline incremental burden (billions of 1988 dollars) (2) | Increase in (billions of 1988 dollars) | | | | Incremental burden (billions of 1988 dollars)[b] (7) |
			GNP (3)	Consumption (4)	OASDI benefits (5)	Net gain[a] (6)	
1986–90	5.3	0.0	0.0	0.0	0.0	0.0	0.0
2000	4.8	-22.9	124.0	-12.4	0.1	-12.5	-10.4
2010	4.9	-23.3	252.5	58.1	5.0	53.2	-76.5
2020	6.2	73.4	354.1	107.0	13.9	93.1	-19.7
2030	7.0	171.1	453.1	148.8	23.6	125.2	45.9
2040	6.9	186.6	571.6	196.7	31.1	165.6	21.0
2050	6.6	192.3	702.4	246.5	38.8	207.7	-15.4
2060	6.5	206.2	861.1	305.8	47.6	258.2	-52.0

Sources: Table 4-1 and authors' calculations as explained in the text.
a. Column 4 minus column 5.
b. Column 2 minus column 6.

Incremental Burden

To measure the burden represented by social security and medicare costs, we have defined a concept of the incremental burden imposed by these programs. In the baseline an increased future burden of social security is evident in the rise above current levels in the share of NNP that must be allocated to benefit payments. In evaluating alternative policies, however, we want to take account of any offsetting increase in the consumption of future generations, above the baseline level, that might be generated by the policy change. Thus, the incremental burden consists of two offsetting components. The first represents the added cost of social security or medicare that results from increases in the ratio of beneficiaries to active workers or from increases in per capita benefits relative to per capita output. The second component is the added income that workers receive because of any policy actions that change per capita output.

In table 4-1 the baseline incremental burden (column 10) is simply the increase above the average of 1986–90 in the share of NNP devoted to OASDI. The introduction of higher saving, however, raises income in future decades out of which the benefits can be paid. Thus, higher OASDI benefits need not reduce the consumption of future workers (see column 11).

Table 4-2 shows how the incremental burden in table 4-1 was calculated. In the baseline projection, OASDI benefits in 2000 and 2010 claim a smaller proportion of output than in the 1986–90 period, but they represent a larger share in subsequent decades (column 1). Thus, measured in dollars the incremental burden (column 2) is negative initially, because of the decline in the ratio of OASDI to NNP. However, the burden rises to $206 billion by 2060.

That burden on future workers can be reduced by increasing national saving today, thus reducing current consumption, and adding to the future stock of capital. The increase in the saving rate by 1.5 percent of GNP would raise output steadily over the period—an increase of $861 billion annually by 2060 (column 3). Increased saving and investment would absorb much of the output gain—reducing consumption until after 2000, but consumption would ultimately rise substantially; the annual gain to consumption would approach $306 billion by 2060 (column 4). The higher stock of capital raises future OASDI benefits (column 5) through its effect on wage rates, but the residual gain in consumption, $258 billion in 2060, more than compensates future generations for the increased burden of social security. The policy benefits future generations after 2000, and the benefits steadily rise until they more than offset the added costs of OASDI after 2040 (column 7). It is this net cost measure of column 7, expressed as a share of NNP, that is shown in column 11 of table 4-1.

These calculations dramatize how today's workers can, through increased saving, spare future generations any added social security burden that otherwise would arise because the baby-boom generation is so large. When medicare expenditures are taken into account in chapter 5, future consumption prospects are not so promising.

The model incorporates two major economic assumptions that have a significant effect on our conclusions. We assume that the private saving rate will not be affected by future changes in interest rates or variations in government saving. And we ignore any induced changes in the supply of labor that might be expected to result from changes in real wage rates. Furthermore, in all of our analyses, change is measured against a single economic baseline, the II-B projections. We examine each of these issues in turn.

Private Saving

The assumption about the behavior of private saving plays a critical role in our analysis of the effects of alternative fiscal policies. Even if social security surpluses are used to increase government saving, they will not translate into greater national saving if they cause private saving to fall.[16] Social security might cause private saving to fall because an increase in government saving will tend to reduce interest

16. In considering this possibility, we take social security benefits as given. This assumption means that most of the research on the effects of social security benefits on saving is not relevant to the question we are examining here. That research typically relates private saving by households or the entire nation to some measure of the present value of promised social security benefits. See Lawrence H. Thompson, "The Social Security Reform Debate," *Journal of Economic Literature*, vol. 21 (December 1983), pp. 1425–67; Henry J. Aaron, *Economic Effects of Social Security* (Brookings, 1982), pp. 40–52; and B. Douglas Bernheim, "The Economic Effects of Social Security: Toward a Reconciliation of Theory and Measurement," *Journal of Public Economics*, vol. 33 (August 1987), pp. 273–304. Analysts could try to estimate the value of such benefits net of anticipated social security taxes, as Martin Feldstein and others have done. Basing estimates on the effect of social security wealth measured without regard for how benefits are financed implies either that the method of finance has no effect on saving apart from the direct effect of taxes on disposable income or that benefits and the taxes necessary to pay for them are uncorrelated.

rates and may thereby discourage private saving,[17] or because decreases in public debt may encourage private consumption. Asking whether the accumulation of social security reserves will affect private saving is therefore equivalent to asking whether the government surplus or deficit affects private saving.

Many analysts would expect future changes in the demographic structure of the population to have important effects on private saving behavior, because individuals exhibit markedly different saving rates at different stages of their lives. The influence of demographics, however, is not critical to our analysis because the focus is on the effects of changes in the the future rate of government saving. Shifts in the age distribution of the population will only alter the baseline projection from which those changes are measured.[18]

Interest Sensitivity of Saving

The simulation reported in table 4-1 highlights the fact that an increase in total saving, if invested domestically, will depress the rate of return to capital and market interest rates. Thus, the possibility that private saving will be reduced by lower interest rates provides one mechanism by which an increase in saving on the part of social security could be offset.

A cloud of uncertainty surrounds estimates of the effects of changes in the net rate of return to saving. Most empirical studies using postwar data suggest that the effects of interest rates on private saving are small.[19] Furthermore, the near elimination of taxation of new saving in the early 1980s had no detectable positive effect on the overall private or personal saving rate.[20] Strong conclusions about the

17. The evidence on whether decreases in interest rates will reduce private saving is ambiguous. See David A. Starrett, "Effects of Taxes on Saving," in Henry J. Aaron, Harvey Galper, and Joseph A. Pechman, eds., *Uneasy Compromise: Problems of a Hybrid Income-Consumption Tax* (Brookings, 1988), pp. 237–59; and Alan J. Auerbach and Laurence J. Kotlikoff, *Dynamic Fiscal Policy* (Cambridge University Press, 1987).

18. The influence of demographic changes is discussed in appendix B.

19. Barry P. Bosworth, *Tax Incentives and Economic Growth* (Brookings, 1984), pp. 59–96.

20. Some studies of household saving behavior conclude that individual retirement accounts (IRAs) added roughly $1 to personal saving for every $2 deposited in IRAs. See Steven F. Venti and David A. Wise, "The Determinants of IRA Contributions and the Effect of Limit Changes," in Zvi Bodie, John B. Shoven, and David A. Wise, eds., *Pensions in the U.S. Economy* (University of Chicago Press, 1988), pp. 9–52; and Steven F. Venti and David A. Wise, "The Evidence on IRAs," *Tax Notes*, vol. 38 (January 25, 1988), pp. 411–16. In the aggregate, however, the U.S. personal

sensitivity of saving to changes in interest rates seem unwarranted, however, because most increases in rates of return have been brief, and the studies of their effects have been based almost exclusively on economywide data. Aggregate data include many groups with potentially divergent behavior. Older groups, who have accumulated assets, will find that their expected future income increases when interest rates rise. Thus they might actually increase their current consumption—reduce their saving—when the after-tax rate of return increases. Young adults, who have few assets and whose behavior will better represent the longer-term responses, are more likely to increase their saving. Even if increased yields could be shown to boost saving in the long run, the decreased saving of the elderly in the short run may outweigh the increased saving of the young.[21]

Despite our skepticism about the impact of interest rates, we did experiment with versions of the model that embodied interest rate effects. When we assume that the interest elasticity of private saving is about 0.4 and allow the private saving rate to decline 1 percentage point for each 1 percentage point fall in market interest rates, the impact on the economy of a change in the rate of government saving is reduced by about half.[22] Because the private saving rate offsets much of the change in social security saving, all of the economic effects are dampened.

Private versus Public Saving

Robert Barro argued in 1974 that government surpluses or deficits cause equal and offsetting changes in private saving, a proposition that Martin J. Bailey had advanced more than a decade earlier.[23] Barro argued that people see their welfare in terms not only of the

---

saving rate fell after 1982, when IRAs were first extended to all wage earners. The net impact of IRAs on personal saving has evidently been quite small or swamped by other factors.

21. See Laurence J. Kotlikoff, "Taxation and Savings: A Neoclassical Perspective," *Journal of Economic Literature*, vol. 22 (December 1984), pp. 1576–1629.

22. The estimate of a 0.4 interest rate elasticity is at the upper end of the range of suggested interest rate effects that can be found in the empirical literature on private saving behavior.

23. Robert J. Barro, "Are Government Bonds Net Wealth?" *Journal of Political Economy*, vol. 82 (November–December 1974), pp. 1095–1117. See also Martin J. Bailey, *National Income and the Price Level: A Study in Macrotheory* (McGraw-Hill, 1962), pp. 154–77.

goods and services they consume, but also of the goods and services that their descendants and heirs will consume. Each generation consumes a portion of its earnings and inheritances and bequeaths the rest. If people are satisfied with the allocation of their wealth between current consumption and bequests, it must mean that at the margin one more dollar of consumption is worth the same as one more dollar of bequest. An increase in the government surplus—for example, from increased social security surpluses—does not change this multigeneration measure of wealth and, according to Barro, should not affect aggregate consumption or its timing.

This line of reasoning leads to the inference that if the government reduces the public debt left to the next generation, private economic agents will restore the preexisting equilibrium by saving less and transferring fewer private assets to the next generation.

Barro's argument, though elegant, has been criticized from a theoretical perspective, and the available statistical evidence is, at best, ambiguous. The conclusion that government saving or dissaving will cause opposite and equal changes in private saving fails if any one of the following assumptions fails to hold.[24] First, the theory fails if consumers are not rational and are not far-sighted. Rationality, in economists' sense of the term, implies that consumers must decide how much to consume on the basis of plans stretching into the infinite future based on expected earnings, interest rates, and tax rates. Second, the theory fails if successive generations are not connected to one another altruistically—altruism meaning that all families in the current generation make bequests and that the motivation for these bequests is the beneficent recognition by the bequeather of the personal satisfaction by heirs that the bequest makes possible. In fact, the motives for bequests are diverse, and many decedents leave none. Third, the theory fails if some people have few assets and cannot borrow to maintain current consumption when taxes rise. Taxes reduce consumption of such households and increase national saving in direct proportion to the consumption of such households.[25]

24. B. Douglas Bernheim, "Ricardian Equivalence: An Evaluation of Theory and Evidence," Working Paper 2330 (Cambridge, Mass.: National Bureau of Economic Research, July 1987), examines the issues outlined here.

25. The theory also could fail if those who pay the initial increase in taxes differ from those who will be spared taxes at some time in the future and if the spending propensities of these two groups differ; if taxes imposed to build up the surplus distort

Furthermore, several empirical studies of the effect of government deficits on private saving suggest that private saving may fall, rather than rise, when government deficits increase. Poterba and Summers find that the large federal deficits since 1982 have coincided with a decrease in private saving, despite sharply increased real interest rates (which should have encouraged private saving).[26] Bernheim finds that most empirical studies reject the proposition that government saving or dissaving causes offsetting changes in private saving. After examining data on changes in government deficits and private saving in twenty-six countries, he concluded that the international evidence is also inconsistent with the Barro hypothesis.[27]

Summers and Carroll have estimated the relationship between national saving, on the one hand, and gross national product, inflation, and capital gains, on the other, for the three decades from 1950 through 1981. If government deficits (which were not included in their regressions) lead to increased private saving, their equations should have predicted less saving than actually occurred during the 1980s. In fact, they predict more private saving than actually occurred from 1982 through 1986.[28]

Both theory and history suggest that increases in government saving will increase national saving. The key to using social security surpluses to add to national saving, therefore, is to make sure that they boost government saving.[29] All of our simulation results reported in chapter

---

economic behavior and change labor supply or saving; or if surpluses cause changes in government spending or taxation (the possibility we raised before). Each of the assumptions about behavior on which the theory depends seems at least a bit far-fetched.

26. James M. Poterba and Lawrence H. Summers, "Recent U.S. Evidence on Budget Deficits and National Savings," Working Paper 2144 (National Bureau of Economic Research, February 1987), and "Finite Lifetimes and the Effects of Budget Deficits on National Saving," *Journal of Monetary Economics*, vol. 20 (September 1987), pp. 369–91.

27. Bernheim, "Ricardian Equivalence."

28. Lawrence Summers and Chris Carroll, "Why Is U.S. National Saving So Low?" *Brookings Papers on Economic Activity*, 2:1987, pp. 607–35. They point out that in 1986 and 1987 private saving fell, thereby adding to the fall-off in national saving, a trend that is opposed to the prediction that increases in government deficits should induce increased private saving.

29. Not all government expenditures that might be financed from the social security reserves should be regarded as consumption. The investment by the federal government of social security reserves in assets that added to the capital stock of the United States and that yielded returns equal to or greater than those that could be generated

5 assume that there is no offsetting change in private saving. It is possible to incorporate such offsets, however, by simply reducing the magnitudes of the numbers—for example, if the private saving response offsets half the change in government saving, the reported changes in the economy and national income should be cut in half.

Labor Supply

In constructing our model we assume that the future labor force and hours worked per person are those of the II-B projections and that they do not change in response to variations in economic factors such as the growth in real wages. We do not believe that the empirical studies of past labor supply behavior support the notion that small variations in real wages will have a major or even predictable effect on labor supply. A rise in the real wage will have both a negative income effect of encouraging workers to take some of their gain in well-being in the form of increased leisure, and a positive substitution effect of increasing the opportunity cost of leisure. Which of the two effects dominates over the long term remains controversial, but in any case the net effect of a small deviation in wages from their baseline path is likely to be inconsequential.

A more pragmatic reason for our assumption is the difficulty of linking variations in labor force participation and future OASDI benefits. Changes in a person's work history will alter the size of the retirement benefit, a complication that would have required substantial disaggregation and introduced additional complexity into our model.

If we had incorporated a labor supply function in which the supply varied positively with real wages, the effects of increased saving on net national product would be increased since the supply of labor would also have been higher. However, because there would be less variation in the capital-labor ratio, the rise in the real wage rate would be smaller. In addition, increases in the supply of labor would reduce the decline in the return to capital that is associated with an increase in capital formation.

Alternative Baseline Assumptions

The specific path of the economy that is used as the baseline for our simulations is not particularly critical to our purpose of evaluating

---

by investments in the private sector would, by definition, add as much to productive capacity as would private investments.

the effects of proposed changes in policy. It is of some interest, however, to use the model to observe the sensitivity of social security to changes in economic conditions. From the perspective of the social security system the critical economic variables are the growth of wages and the level of the real interest rate. Both taxes and benefits are tied directly to covered wages; if wage growth increases, the financial health of the system improves because increased wages raise taxes before benefits. The real interest rate determines how much the trust funds will earn from the sizable reserves they are projected to accumulate.

Productivity Growth

The future growth of taxable earnings is determined by (1) the rate of growth of total factor productivity (technical change); (2) growth in the supply of labor hours—which is based on projections of future population, labor force participation rates, and hours worked per person per year—and (3) changes in the proportion of labor compensation provided in the form of fringe benefits, which are not included in the calculation of either OASDHI taxes or benefits.

The 1986 II-B projections were based on an optimistic assumption, relative to recent trends, about the growth of productivity. Implicitly, they assumed that total factor productivity in the nonfarm business sector will rise at an annual average rate of 1.4 percent over the 1985–2060 period. That is equal to the actual rate over the 1950–1973 period; but, for the longer span of 1950–1985, the actual rate was only 1.0 percent, and it was a dismal 0.4 percent annually between 1973 and 1985.[30]

In the 1986 report the effect of the optimistic assumption about productivity growth was moderated by projections that both the number of hours worked per person and the share of money wages in total compensation would decline substantially in future decades. Both of these assumptions operated to limit the growth in wages covered by the OASDI program. By 1988, the annual trustees' report had reduced the projected growth of productivity but had offset those changes by revised estimates of the growth of fringe benefits and the length of the work week. The result was a very modest reduction in the assumed long-run growth of real wages.[31]

30. The calculations use an average of 1973 and 1974 to avoid the strong cyclical distortions of that period.

31. Revisions in the II-B projections are discussed in chapter 3 and appendix A.

FIGURE 4-1. **Net National Product under Three Productivity Assumptions, 1986–2060**

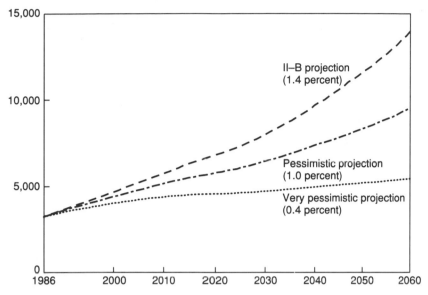

Billions of 1982 dollars

Source: Authors' calculations based on unpublished data from the Social Security Administration.

We examined the effects of more dramatic changes in productivity growth, one a moderately pessimistic projection in which total factor productivity growth averages 1.0 percent annually, and the other a very pessimistic projection in which the growth rate is cut to 0.4 percent annually. When compounded over seventy-five years these seemingly small changes in annual growth rates have very large economic effects, as figure 4-1 shows.

The result of the moderately pessimistic assumption is to lower net national product, consumption, and real wages by 32 percent in 2060 relative to the baseline. The social security fund experiences a major deterioration as benefits, lagging behind the change in wages, are reduced by 26 percent in 2060 while revenues are down 32 percent. The trust fund reserve reaches its peak as a share of NNP at 25 percent in 2016, compared to 32 percent in 2019 for the baseline, and the reserve is exhausted under currently scheduled tax rates by 2037, instead of around 2050. By 2060 the OASDI trust fund has a debt equal to 44 percent of NNP. Under the very pessimistic assumption, NNP in

2060 is only 68 percent above its actual 1986 level (adjusted for inflation). In addition, the surplus of OASDI is highly transitory, reaching a peak accumulation equal to 15 percent of NNP in 2013; it is exhausted in 2026.

Obviously, the assumed rate of productivity growth is critical for any evaluation of the financial condition of social security and the magnitude of any surplus that will accumulate over the next few decades. However, the economic evaluation is limited by the failure to incorporate into the simulation the necessity for future tax rate increases and their effects on the economy. (The implications for financing social security and for the burden that the system will impose on future workers are considered in greater detail in chapter 5.)

Interest Rates

The II-B projections assume that the real rate of interest earned by the OASDI trust fund will decline to 2 percent by the mid-1990s and remain at that level. We experimented with an alternative projection in which the interest rate earned on the fund is raised by 1 percentage point throughout the entire forecast period. While the structure of the model in the baseline simulation implies that the change would have no effect on the path of the real economy because changes in social security saving are simply absorbed by offsetting changes in the rest of the federal budget, the reduced interest rate alters the financial status of OASDI and the need for additional tax increases.

With a higher level of interest income, the trust fund continues to have a positive reserve throughout the period. The reserve reaches a peak equal to 37 percent of NNP in 2025; and at the end of the simulation period, 2060, the reserve is 5 percent of NNP compared to a net debt of 11 percent of NNP in the baseline. In addition, if we compute, as in chapter 3, the tax-rate increases needed to keep the funds in close actuarial balance, those increases are much smaller than those needed in the baseline, and they occur later. The higher interest earnings replace some of the payroll tax revenue that would otherwise be needed to keep the funds solvent.

In the past, interest rates were not an important element in projections of the funds' financial condition because the funds did not accumulate large reserves. That is no longer true because of the decision to depart from pay-as-you-go financing. Unfortunately, the economic basis for making projections of future interest rates is extremely weak.

CHAPTER 5

The Burden of Social Security and Medicare

THIS CHAPTER examines the effects of various policies for financing social security on national income and the social security system.[1] The model is based on the 1986 II-B demographic and economic projections of the social security trustees.[2] It contains an initial baseline projection of the path of the economy out to 2060 in which the total federal deficit equals 1.5 percent of gross national product (GNP) each year. That assumption implies that the surpluses of the old-age, survivors, and disability insurance (OASDI) and hospital insurance (HI) trust funds are offset by a correspondingly larger deficit on other government operations.[3]

The model is used to contrast the economic outcome in the baseline case with the economic outcome when national saving is increased. When the baseline assumption about fiscal policy is changed to one in which the non-OASDI deficit is held at 1.5 percent of GNP, any social security surpluses add to national saving. Thus, relative to the baseline, the OASDI surplus is set aside as increased national saving rather than being used to finance expenditures in other government accounts.

The effects of the change turn out to depend on whether all of the

1. On this issue see John C. Hambor, "Economic Policy, Intergenerational Equity and the Social Security Trust Fund Buildup," *Social Security Bulletin*, October 1987, pp. 13–18; Alicia H. Munnell and Lynn E. Blais, "Do We Want Larger Social Security Surpluses?" *New England Economic Review* (September–October 1984), pp. 5–21; and Joseph M. Anderson, *Revised Phase II Report: Analysis of the Economic Effects of OASDI Trust Fund Growth under Alternative Federal Budget Scenarios*, Report submitted by ICF Inc. to U.S. Department of Health and Human Services, Social Security Administration, September 1987.

2. *1986 Annual Report of the Board of Trustees of the Federal Old-Age and Survivors Insurance and Disability Insurance [OASDI] Trust Funds* (Baltimore, Md.: Social Security Administration, 1986).

3. In the past the long-run target for the budget deficit was zero, but economic and political events consistently caused performance to fall short of the target. In effect, by assuming an average deficit of 1.5 percent of GNP we are assuming that this same discrepancy between targets and performance will continue in the future.

76

increased saving is invested domestically or some of it flows abroad, possibilities that are evaluated separately.[4] Finally, we include the hospital insurance portion of medicare and evaluate the effects on the economy of increasing saving by the amounts that will be accumulated in the HI trust fund if medicare taxes are set at rates sufficient to keep the medicare system in close actuarial balance.[5] The chapter concludes with an evaluation of the policy of saving the surplus when assumptions about future productivity are less optimistic than those of the II-B projections.

All of the simulations assume that the OASDI tax rates are permanently increased in the year following a determination that the fund has moved out of close balance over a seventy-five-year horizon. The amount of tax increase is sufficient to restore actuarial balance measured over the succeeding seventy-five years. This is the periodically adjusted level tax policy that is discussed more fully in chapter 3. Because the rising number of projected beneficiaries generates increasing costs, this policy assumption implies a buildup of reserves much larger than those projected under current law. A pay-as-you-go system that incorporates a series of future tax rate increases can be actuarially balanced, but it will generate no surpluses.[6]

The policies evaluated in this chapter entail no change in social security benefit formulas. Rather they concern the fiscal operations of the rest of the federal government and the revenues of the OASDHI system. Whether surpluses of the social security system are set aside to add to national saving or borrowed to finance other government programs has little direct effect on social security balance. The system will have access to accumulated reserves in either case, but if the funds simply finance consumption-type expenditures in other government accounts, they will not have changed the nation's rate of saving, capital formation, or future income. In the context of the model, a policy of saving the surplus requires that other government expenditures be reduced or other taxes be increased to produce a non-OASDI budget deficit of 1.5 percent of GNP.

4. If saving flows abroad, the United States will run a current account surplus with the rest of the world.

5. Close actuarial balance, as defined in chapter 3, is measured over a twenty-five-year horizon, in contrast to the seventy-five-year horizon used for social security.

6. We experimented with delaying any required tax increase for up to twenty years. The delay changed the timing of the increments to saving but the cumulative amount remained about the same. We adopted the rule of an immediate tax increase only because it yields the smallest required magnitude of tax change.

TABLE 5-1. **Economic Effects of Investing Domestically the Social Security Trust Fund Surplus under a Periodically Adjusted Level Tax Schedule, Selected Years, 1990–2060**

Year	General economy (percent change from baseline)					Social security (percent change from baseline)				Incremental burden (percent of NNP)[a]	
	Capital stock (1)	Net national product (2)	Consumption[b] (3)	Wage rate (4)	Nominal interest rate[c] (5)	Payroll taxes (6)	Benefits (7)	Interest receipts[d] (8)	Trust fund reserve[e] (9)	Baseline (10)	Higher saving (11)
1990	0.0	0.0	0.0	0.0	0.0	0.0	0.0	0.0	0.0	−0.1	−0.1
2000	9.4	1.8	−0.8	3.1	−0.14	8.8	0.4	3.6	4.3	−0.4	0.3
2010	19.6	3.6	0.8	6.1	−0.49	12.0	2.6	6.4	9.2	−0.3	−1.0
2020	23.7	4.2	2.6	7.1	−0.74	20.2	5.0	8.7	14.3	1.0	−1.2
2030	21.0	3.9	3.6	6.3	−0.79	19.3	6.2	13.3	19.2	1.8	−1.2
2040	16.2	3.2	3.0	4.9	−0.64	17.7	6.0	19.2	22.9	1.6	−0.8
2050	13.4	2.6	2.1	4.1	−0.51	23.8	5.3	26.4	28.4	1.4	−0.2
2060	12.4	2.5	2.0	3.8	−0.46	23.5	4.6	36.9	37.0	1.2	−0.3

Source: Authors' calculations as explained in the text.

a. The increase in the ratio of old-age, survivors, and disability insurance (OASDI) benefits to baseline net national product (NNP) from the 1986–90 average, minus the increase in consumption from the baseline level, expressed as a percent of NNP in the baseline.

b. Private consumption plus all government expenditures (includes government investment-type outlays).

c. Expressed as the simple difference from the baseline in percentage points.

d. Expressed as a percent of total OASDI income.

e. Expressed as a percent of NNP in the baseline.

Our results indicate that the added future consumption that results from saving and investing today's social security surplus is more than enough to offset all of the increased burden on future workers of providing pensions for a larger population of retirees. The benefits of this policy in the form of increased wages and consumption, made possible by a larger capital stock, exceed the added costs of social security benefit payments. In the case of medicare, the added consumption from saving the surplus largely offsets, but does not completely eliminate, the burden on future workers of paying for sharply higher HI benefits. Finally, if the added saving is invested abroad, rather than in the United States, it will still increase U.S. incomes and consumption, but the added saving will not raise domestic wage rates and thus it will not affect future benefits of social security recipients. The additions to national income would accrue to the United States in the form of higher capital income from the rest of the world.

The Effects of Accumulating Reserves

Our assumption in the baseline projection that the government always runs total budget deficits of 1.5 percent of GNP implies that any changes in the surpluses or deficits of the social security system are offset by equal and opposite changes in the balances of other government accounts. The policy is economically equivalent to accumulating no surplus at all because social security is included in the total budget. In other words, the choice of tax schedules to finance social security has no effect on fiscal policy if the resulting surpluses and deficits are just offset by other government operations.[7]

Increased Saving Invested Domestically

Table 5-1 illustrates the economic effects of a policy in which social security taxes are increased as necessary to keep the OASDI trust fund in close actuarial balance and in which fiscal policy is managed so that all social security surpluses result in added national saving. The non-OASDI budget deficit is set equal to 1.5 percent of GNP, the level of the overall deficit in the baseline case.

7. The incidence of payroll taxes differs from that of other government taxes. To the extent that the economic effects of the federal budget depend on tax incidence, the composition of government revenues will have some effect on economic activity. We ignore such effects in the results reported below.

FIGURE 5-1. **Social Security Tax Rates under Current Law and a Periodically Adjusted Level Tax Schedule, 1986–2060**

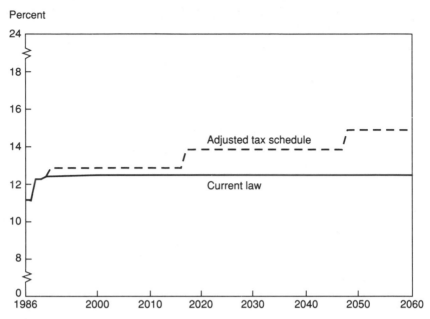

Percent

Sources: *Economic Projections for OASDHI Cost and Income Estimates, 1986,* Actuarial Study 98 (Baltimore, Md.: Social Security Administration, 1987); SSA, Office of Actuary, unpublished data; and authors' calculations.

The tax rates that achieve actuarial balance under this assumption are shown in figure 5-1. This schedule closely resembles the schedule shown in figure 3-3. The two schedules are not identical, however. The adjusted rates in this chapter take account of the effect of added saving on earnings and interest rates, which in turn affect social security's financial position and hence the timing and size of tax increases necessary to maintain actuarial balance.[8] This tax schedule leads to the accumulation of significantly larger reserves than those in the baseline projection, especially in the later years of the simulation (column 9, table 5-1).

The simulation results summarized in table 5-1 compare the levels

8. In each year of the simulation the trustees are assumed to make a new seventy-five-year projection based on the tax rates of that year. The economic effects of any tax change required to maintain close actuarial balance are not included in the derivation of the magnitude of the required increase; if the feedback effect had been included, the magnitude of each tax increase would be slightly smaller.

of key economic variables with those that would result if all social security surpluses were offset by increased deficits elsewhere in the federal budget or, equivalently, if no trust fund accumulation occurred, as under pay-as-you-go taxation.[9]

The results of changing national saving by the amount of social security trust fund accumulation or decumulation are qualitatively similar to those shown in chapter 4 when national saving was raised by a constant 1.5 percent of gross national product.[10] As a result of the increased investment, the capital stock, labor productivity, and real wages all rise. The rate of return to capital falls, however. The decline in the rate of return is caused by the increased supply of capital, which causes savings to be invested in projects with progressively lower returns. The rate of return is inversely related to the ratio of capital to output. In the model we assume that monetary policy will be adjusted to reduce the cost of borrowing by an amount that is proportionate to the decline in the rate of return. This easing of monetary policy is a necessary offset to the tighter fiscal policy implied by smaller overall budget deficits.

Net national product rises 4.2 percent by 2020 and 2.5 percent by 2060 (column 2). Consumption initially declines because of the increased rate of saving and investment; but by 2010, the extra output generated by the added capital is sufficient to raise consumption above the baseline level; the percentage gain reaches a peak of 3.6 percent in 2030 (column 3).

Because the increase in saving derives, in part, from increased payroll taxes, the effects on the social security system are unambiguously favorable. Tax revenues rise sharply because of both the higher tax rates required to maintain close actuarial balance and the increase in taxable earnings induced by the larger capital stock.[11] Benefits also

9. Although the effects on the economy of these two policies are identical, the effects on the social security system are quite different; no sizable trust fund accumulation occurs under the pay-as-you-go policy.

10. The difference is that the increment to national saving rises steadily to 2.2 percent of GNP in 2000, reaches a peak of 2.8 percent in 2010, and then declines to 1.0 percent by 2060. If all saving is invested domestically, the capital stock increases sharply after 1990, cumulating to a capital stock 23.7 percent larger than in the baseline case by 2020 and 12.4 percent larger by 2060 (column 1).

11. To maintain actuarial balance under the assumption that the social security surplus is saved and domestically invested, payroll tax rates must be raised by 0.7 percent in 1991, by 0.8 percent in 2017, and by 0.8 percent in 2048. The situation

increase, but by a much smaller amount that reflects only the delayed response to higher real wages.

Perhaps the most striking change is in the pattern of trust fund accumulation. Rather than rising and then falling, as it would under the current tax schedule, the trust fund reserve remains positive throughout the next seventy-five years. At the end of the projection period it is larger than in the baseline case by an amount greater than one-third of net national product (column 9).

The most important results concern the incremental burden of social security.[12] In the case where government and national saving remains at historical averages (the baseline), the burden of social security on the economy rises by a maximum of 1.8 percent of net national product in 2030 and by 1.2 percent in 2060. If fiscal policy is managed so that social security surpluses increase national saving, the incremental burden essentially vanishes (column 11). The extra future consumption made possible by the increase in the capital stock exceeds the increased burden of social security. In other words, under a policy of boosting payroll taxes whenever social security slips out of close actuarial balance and managing fiscal policy so that the surpluses add to national saving, social security pension benefits will impose no additional burden whatsoever on future generations who are active participants in the work force. Instead, the initial sacrifice, in the form of reduced consumption, is made by the workers who receive the future benefits, and the earnings from their added saving are sufficient to pay the added costs of their retirement.

Increased Saving Invested Abroad

The results in table 5-1 indicate that the extra costs of social security for a growing population of beneficiaries can be offset by the added national income that increased saving will generate. But these same results indicate that additional saving will cause the marginal productivity of capital invested in the United States to fall below its baseline value. At its low point in 2026 the net before-tax return to physical capital would be only 3.6 percent, compared to a 1986–90 average of 8.9 percent.[13] The rate of return to investment falls because of a large

---

in which the system is in actuarial surplus, justifying a tax reduction, did not arise over the simulation period.

12. The concept of incremental burden is explained in chapter 4.

13. By net before-tax return we mean the return to capital after subtracting capital depreciation and indirect business taxes but before subtracting corporate or personal

increase in the ratio of capital to labor. Although the growth of the labor force is projected to slow dramatically—from an average of 1.8 percent per year from 1950 through 1985 to an average of only 0.3 percent per year over the next seventy-five years—we assumed that the historical rates of private saving and investment will be maintained. As a result, the amount of capital per worker will grow sharply. Unless the rate of technological advance rises to levels unprecedented in recent U.S. history, this sharp increase in the capital-labor ratio must depress the rate of return.

Faced with such a sharp drop in the domestic rate of return, U.S. savers would look abroad for more attractive investment possibilities. The growth of the labor force in other developed industrial countries is also slowing, however, and those countries also may experience falling rates of return. For this reason few opportunities may exist for U.S. investors to earn higher rates of return in the developed world than they can at home. Whether the newly industrializing and underdeveloped countries will provide a sufficient outlet for U.S. saving, and possibly that of other developed nations, is impossible to forecast. It is important, however, to examine the implications for the American economy and for the social security system if U.S. saving rises and part or all of the increase flows abroad.

To facilitate understanding of the economic effects of foreign capital flows, we present the results in two stages. First, we modify the baseline simulation by assuming that saving will be invested abroad whenever the domestic after-tax rate of return on physical capital falls below the average yield from 1986 to 1990. Then we examine the effects of adjusting payroll taxes to maintain continuous close actuarial balance, pursuing a fiscal policy that translates these surpluses into increased national saving, and investing the added saving overseas.

We assume in computing the income generated by foreign investment that it earns a constant rate of return equal to 7.3 percent, a rate midway between the before- and after-corporate-tax rate of return in the United States over the period 1986–1990. In deriving this alternative baseline simulation, we continued to use currently sched-

---

income taxes. Our measure, which is somewhat unconventional, magnifies the decline in the rate of return. Although land is included, as a fixed amount, in the broad definition of capital used to project nonfarm business output, we did not have a means of valuing it in the future. Thus, we excluded land from the denominator in calculating the gross rate of return, yielding an artificially high value. The broader measure would probably decline less than ours does.

TABLE 5-2. **Economic Effects of International Capital Flows, Selected Years, 1990–2060**

Percent change from baseline

Year	General economy					Social security			
	Capital stock (1)	Net national product (2)	Consumption (3)	Wage rate (4)	Nominal interest rate[a] (5)	Payroll taxes (6)	Benefits (7)	Interest receipts[b] (8)	Trust fund reserve[c] (9)
1990	−0.1	−0.1	n.a.	0.0	−0.01	0.0	0.0	−0.04	0.0
2000	−9.2	−0.8	n.a.	−3.3	0.15	−3.3	−0.5	−0.7	−1.0
2010	−17.3	−1.5	n.a.	−6.2	0.49	−6.2	−2.7	−1.1	−2.7
2020	−26.6	−2.3	n.a.	−9.9	0.94	−9.9	−5.6	−0.2	−3.8
2030	−30.5	−2.6	n.a.	−11.4	1.35	−11.4	−8.4	1.2	−3.0
2040	−30.9	−2.8	n.a.	−11.5	1.41	−11.5	−10.0	1.2	−1.1
2050	−32.0	−2.9	n.a.	−11.9	1.46	−11.9	−10.9	0.2	0.1
2060	−32.0	−3.0	n.a.	−11.9	1.49	−11.9	−11.4	−2.3	0.2

Source: Authors' calculations as explained in the text.

n.a. Not available.

a. Expressed as the simple difference from the baseline in percentage points.

b. Expressed as a percent of total OASDI income.

c. Expressed as a percent of NNP in the baseline.

uled payroll tax rates for OASDI and to assume that any surplus or deficit in social security leaves the overall government deficit unchanged.

As shown in table 5-2, the shift of capital to the international market lowers U.S. NNP below its baseline level (column 2). Net national product drops because we assumed that the private rate of return on foreign capital is less than the rate of return on capital invested in the United States. The return on foreign investment is substantially below the contribution to output of capital in the United States because it excludes capital income taxes that accrue to foreign governments.[14]

In addition, when capital is invested domestically the benefits of increased income are divided between an increase in profit income and a rise in domestic wages. Workers gain from the increase in productivity that is made possible by increased capital per worker. When U.S. saving flows abroad the earnings of Americans are raised only by the gain in profit income—the wages of American workers are not increased.

Finally, the initial outflow of capital from the United States will lower the U.S. terms of trade—export prices must fall relative to import prices to induce foreigners to buy more than they sell to the United States. This effect on the terms of trade and real living standards of Americans will be reversed when the income from the investments flows back into the United States. These complex effects on the terms of trade are not incorporated into the model simulations; and the reported results are very dependent on our assumptions. Our results should be interpreted only as illustrative of a situation of open international capital markets.

The potential for international capital flows, however, does have dramatic implications for the domestic economy. First, to the extent that capital flows abroad, the domestic capital stock is smaller and U.S. real wages lower than in the baseline case. In our alternative baseline simulation, the capital stock is reduced by 30.5 percent by 2030, and real wages fall 11.4 percent below the baseline in which all saving is domestically invested. The drop in wage income reflects

14. In addition, we assumed that the capital outflow is a small portion of the rest-of-world capital stock, and that an increase in U.S. investment abroad does not depress the foreign rate of return as it would if it were invested in the United States. The use of the average of the before- and after-tax rates of return can be viewed as a partial allowance for the extra risk of foreign investment.

the reduction in the capital-labor ratio and, thus, in labor productivity. Second, both social security taxes and benefits (columns 6 and 7) are lower than in the baseline case, because they are tied to wage income, not national income.

We are conceptually unable to calculate the effect on consumption of the change in capital allocation. The U.S. national accounts do not include in GNP a capital consumption allowance (depreciation) for capital invested overseas. Thus, when capital is reallocated from the domestic to the foreign sector, the reported level of GNP declines. Because we measure consumption (public plus private) by subtracting gross investment from GNP, any misstatement of GNP translates into a corresponding mismeasurement of consumption. The same problem prevents the calculation of the incremental burden.

Although the consequences for consumption are difficult to derive exactly, the general character of the effects of foreign investment can be inferred from table 5-2. The change in consumption arising from investment abroad must be qualitatively similar to the change in net national product (column 2). In addition, the future burden of social security is lower when part of national saving is invested abroad than when it is entirely invested in the United States. This follows from the fact that social security taxes and benefits fall by proportionately larger amounts than NNP (compare columns 6 and 7 with column 2).

To calculate the effects of saving the surplus when the increased saving is invested abroad, we again assume that tax rates are increased as necessary to maintain actuarial balance, and that the deficit in the non-OASDI budget is held at 1.5 percent of GNP.[15] We do not present a detailed table of the results because there will be no effect on the domestic capital stock and real wages; and, therefore, there is no effect on the financial position of the social security trust fund— benefits and taxes are unchanged. The added overseas investment will increase net national product in future years when the income earned on that investment is returned to the United States. In contrast to the situation in which the saving is invested domestically, the gain in NNP is smaller because the U.S. economy as a whole benefits less from increased foreign investment; there is no direct gain to American workers. If the foreign investment earned a 7.3 percent rate of return, NNP would be increased by 2.4 percent in 2020 in comparison to 4.2

15. The specific tax rate increases are 0.75 percent in 2009 and 0.82 percent in 2044. The required tax rate increases are smaller than for the case reported in table 5-1 because the funds are earning a much higher rate of interest.

percent if the saving was invested domestically. The corresponding gains in NNP in 2060 are 1.4 percent if investment flows abroad and 2.5 percent if it does not.

Even if added saving flows abroad, it adds to net national product; but the gain accrues as added capital income, not as increased labor earnings. Added saving will reduce the future burden of social security because it raises NNP without affecting future social security benefits. If one's sole objective were to reduce the social security burden on future generations, foreign investment might be preferred over domestic investment of the extra saving because there would be no induced increase in social security benefits. A foreign outlet for saving also reduces any tendency for increased saving to depress the domestic U.S. rate of return to capital.

Foreign investment of all added saving should be viewed as an extreme case that highlights the important changes that open international capital markets engender. The capital outflow is enormous and it is the opposite of recent experience in which the United States has been borrowing from other countries.[16]

The Cost of Medicare

Currently legislated taxes are grossly insufficient to meet the long-term costs of medicare hospital benefits. The payroll taxes necessary to bring the hospital insurance program into close actuarial balance will be sizable.[17] Figure 5-2 shows how the rates needed to keep the HI program actuarially balanced over a twenty-five-year planning horizon compare with the currently legislated rates.[18]

As with social security pensions, balance could be achieved with pay-as-you-go financing. If the pay-as-you-go option were chosen for both social security pensions and medicare, the two programs would

16. If the sign of some of the numbers in table 5-2 is reversed to reflect a flow of foreign capital into the United States, the funds borrowed from abroad actually raise future social security benefits and taxes by making possible the financing of capital projects that the United States could not afford if it had to rely on its own saving.

17. As with the simulations of OASDI alone, the tax rates used in this analysis differ slightly from those of chapter 3 because they reflect the effects of changes in taxable wages and interest rates on the financial position of the trust funds.

18. The twenty-five-year horizon for evaluating actuarial balance is adopted only because the HI trustees and Congress traditionally evaluate the solvency of the HI program over a shorter time horizon than is used in the OASDI program. If a seventy-five-year horizon had been used, the required HI tax increases over the next two decades would be much greater than shown in figure 5-2. The HI trust fund buildup and the reduction in the future burden would consequently be much larger as well.

TABLE 5-3. **Economic Effects of Investing Domestically the Social Security and Hospital Insurance Trust Fund Surplus under a Periodically Adjusted Level Tax Schedule, Selected Years, 1990–2060**

| Year | General economy (percent change from baseline) | | | | | Social security and hospital insurance (percent change from baseline) | | | | Incremental burden (percent of NNP)[a] | |
	Capital stock (1)	Net national product (2)	Consumption[b] (3)	Wage rate (4)	Nominal interest rate[c] (5)	Payroll taxes (6)	Benefits (7)	Interest receipts[d] (8)	Trust fund reserve[e] (9)	Baseline (10)	Higher saving (11)
1990	3.0	0.6	-0.5	1.0	-0.04	7.1	0.0	2.5	2.1	-0.1	0.4
2000	14.4	2.7	-0.4	4.6	-0.27	11.0	1.0	6.1	7.4	-0.0	0.3
2010	26.0	4.6	1.1	7.9	-0.65	14.4	3.8	8.6	12.7	0.3	-0.5
2020	32.4	5.5	3.2	9.5	-0.95	23.6	6.8	12.1	20.0	2.1	-0.6
2030	28.4	5.1	4.9	8.3	-1.01	22.2	8.2	15.8	24.2	3.5	-0.4
2040	21.3	4.0	4.2	6.3	-0.81	20.0	8.0	21.5	26.8	3.5	0.2
2050	16.6	3.2	2.8	5.0	-0.64	25.6	6.9	28.2	31.2	3.2	1.1
2060	14.5	2.9	2.3	4.4	-0.54	24.9	5.8	38.7	39.3	3.0	1.2

Source: Authors' calculations as explained in the text.
a. The increase in the ratio of OASDI and hospital insurance (HI) benefits to baseline NNP from the 1986–90 average, minus the increase in consumption from the baseline level, expressed as a percent of NNP in the baseline.
b. Private consumption plus all government expenditures (includes government investment-type outlays).
c. Expressed as the simple difference from the baseline in percentage points.
d. Expressed as a percent of total OASDHI income.
e. Expressed as a percent of NNP in the baseline.

FIGURE 5-2. **Medicare and Combined Social Security and Medicare Tax Rates under Current Law and a Periodically Adjusted Level Tax Schedule, 1986–2060**

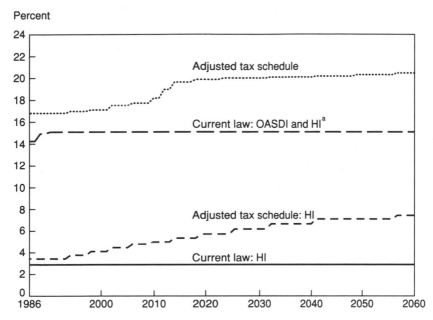

Percent

Sources: OASDHI Economic Projections, 1986; SSA, Office of the Actuary, unpublished data; and authors' calculations using the 1986 Annual Report of the Board of Trustees of the Federal Hospital Insurance Trust Fund (U.S. Department of Health and Human Services, Health Care Financing Administration, 1986).
a. Old-age, survivors, and disability insurance and hospital insurance.

impose an incremental burden that reaches a maximum of 3.5 percent of net national product in 2030 before falling to 3.0 percent in 2060 (table 5-3, column 10).

If, instead, payroll taxes for both medicare and social security pensions are increased whenever either program slips out of close actuarial balance by enough to restore balance, the tax schedule would follow the pattern shown in figure 5-2 and large reserves would accumulate in the trust fund. As with social security pensions viewed in isolation, the medicare trust fund would have negligible economic effect unless it added to national saving. The practical question is whether such savings would be sufficient to offset the sizable incremental burdens that will result under pay-as-you-go financing.

Table 5-3 answers this question. The answer is "yes" between 2010 and 2030, but "not quite" from 2040 on (column 11). The combination of social security pensions and medicare hospital benefits will reduce consumption for the rest of the population by a maximum of about 1.2 percent in 2060 (column 11). These results, based on the assumption that all saving is invested domestically, are comparable to those in table 5-1 but not to those in table 5-2.

Because medicare payroll taxes must be raised sharply and promptly if the goal is to restore the program to close actuarial balance, large additions to national saving will result if the increases in reserves are not offset by deficits in other government operations. The capital stock initially grows much faster than in the baseline simulation or in the case where reserves are saved only for social security pensions. The increase in saving and investment in the short run reduces consumption until after 2000; but the long-run gain (column 3) is greater than in the simulation shown in table 5-1. By 2020 the capital stock is 32.4 percent larger than in the baseline case and 7.0 percent larger than it is when saving rises only by the additions to social security reserves. This difference narrows in the remainder of the projection period because of increased capital consumption. The larger capital stock raises national income above the baseline projection, thus sharply reducing the burden on the economy of providing for social security and medicare benefits.

Because the rise in the capital stock is greater than in the case where only the social security reserve is saved, all of the effects that flow from an increased capital stock are also magnified. Real wage growth is accelerated, and the drop in the rate of return is magnified. Payroll tax revenues and social security benefits are both increased. We assume, optimistically, that wage increases do not cause any change in medicare payments.[19]

Under currently scheduled tax rates, deficits in the hospital insurance trust fund overwhelm surpluses in the social security pension trust funds by 2026. If taxes are increased whenever either system slips out of close actuarial balance, the combined trust funds grow continuously over the entire seventy-five-year projection horizon. In contrast, current official projections indicate that OASDI reserves will be exhausted around 2050 and HI reserves in 2005.[20] Furthermore, a

19. In reality, medicare payments cover hospitalization costs, which will surely rise if real wage levels increase.

20. *1988 OASDI Annual Report*, p. 141; and *1988 Annual Report of the Board of Trustees of the Federal Hospital Insurance Trust Fund* (Washington, D.C.: U.S. Department of Health and Human Services, Health Care Financing Administration, 1988), p. 49.

policy of increasing national saving by the additions to OASDI and HI reserves is sufficient to offset most, but not all, of the combined burdens of OASDI pensions and HI hospital benefits. As table 5-3, column 11, indicates, the increment to total consumption from investing the additions to reserves of both programs exceeds the added cost of benefits from before 2020 to some time after 2030.

The Effects of Slower Productivity Growth

One of the central assumptions of our baseline model is that future productivity will follow the path projected by the OASDI trustees under the intermediate, II-B assumptions of the 1986 report.[21] The growth of total factor productivity implicit in the II-B assumptions is much higher than actual increases observed since the first oil price shock in 1973. Chapter 4 describes the implications for future national income and the OASDI trust fund of slower rates of total factor productivity growth when the overall government deficit—including OASDI—is assumed to remain a fixed, 1.5 percent share of GNP. This section reports estimates of the effects of slower productivity growth when fiscal policy seeks instead to raise national saving by the amount of the OASDI surplus.

Again the three alternative rates of total factor productivity growth considered here are the 1.4 percent annual rate assumed under the 1986 II-B projection; a rate of 1.0 percent per year, corresponding to actual productivity growth from 1950 through 1985; and a rate of 0.4 percent per year, corresponding to actual productivity growth from 1973 through 1985. The lower the growth of productivity, the higher the tax rate required to pay for currently scheduled benefits. Figure 5-3 shows the payroll tax rates that would be required for a strict pay-as-you-go OASDI program under each of the three productivity growth assumptions. For purposes of comparison, the currently scheduled tax rate is also shown. If productivity grows at the rate assumed in the II-B projection, the required pay-as-you-go tax rate would reach 15 percent by 2030 and stabilize thereafter. Under the very pessimistic productivity assumption the rate would reach nearly 18.3 percent by 2030 and rise gradually to 19 percent over the next three decades. Tax rates would rise much earlier under a system where the trust fund is kept in close actuarial balance and the payroll tax is raised in the year after the fund falls out of close actuarial balance, that is,

21. *1986 OASDI Annual Report.*

TABLE 5-4. **Growth of Net Real Wages under Varying Assumptions about Productivity Growth and Fiscal Policy, Selected Years, 1986–2060**[a]

1985 = 100

Year	Productivity growth of 1.4 percent[b]			Productivity growth of 1.0 percent			Productivity growth of 0.4 percent		
	Pay-as-you-go (1)	Base-line (2)	Increased saving (3)	Pay-as-you-go (4)	Base-line (5)	Increased saving (6)	Pay-as-you-go (7)	Base-line (8)	Increased saving (9)
1986	100	100	100	100	99	98	99	97	97
1990	112	110	110	109	107	107	105	102	103
2000	135	131	135	126	122	127	113	109	115
2010	165	160	170	145	142	151	121	117	126
2020	199	198	211	166	165	179	127	127	138
2030	241	244	259	190	193	206	133	135	146
2040	297	299	314	221	223	235	142	144	153
2050	365	368	380	257	259	271	151	154	161
2060	449	450	467	298	301	313	161	163	171

Source: Authors' calculations as explained in the text.
a. Net real wage is compensation per manhour, including fringe benefits, after subtracting the OASDI payroll tax, adjusted for changes in the weighted consumer price index.
b. The assumed rate of growth in total factor productivity that underlies the II-B projections and the baseline projections of our model averages 1.4 percent annually.

FIGURE 5-3. **Pay-as-You-Go Tax Rates for Social Security under Three Productivity Growth Rates, 1986–2060**

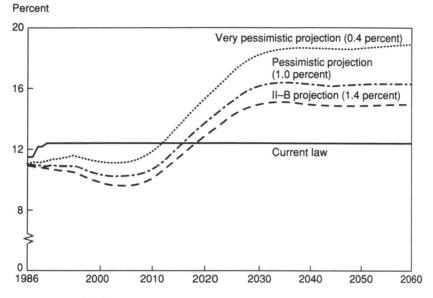

Percent

Source: Authors' calculations based on unpublished data from the Social Security Administration.

under our periodically adjusted level tax policy. However, the general pattern would be the same as that shown in figure 5-3. Taxes would rise much more sharply under a pessimistic productivity assumption than under an optimistic one.

Slow productivity growth retards growth of workers' net real compensation per hour for two reasons. Growth of gross compensation per hour is reduced because growth in real output per hour falls. In addition, the growth in after-tax labor compensation falls even further because it is subject to increased tax rates to pay for OASDI benefits. Table 5-4 shows the combined impact of various tax and fiscal policies and productivity growth rates on the growth of net wages. The first three columns show the future trend in net compensation under the II-B assumptions adopted in 1986. Column 1 shows net compensation growth under a strict pay-as-you-go tax formula. Column 2 shows the trend under the periodically adjusted level tax schedule when the social security surplus does not add to national saving (our baseline assumption regarding fiscal policy).[22] The compensation trend in column 3 is calculated under the alternative fiscal assumption that the social security surplus adds to national saving. Because the capital stock is higher under the alternative fiscal policy (table 5-1), both worker productivity and net compensation are increased. By 2030, net compensation under the alternative fiscal policy is about 6 percent higher than it would be under the baseline policy; by 2060, it is about 4 percent higher.

Columns 4 through 6 in table 5-4 show trends in net compensation under the alternative tax formulas and fiscal policies when we adopt the assumption that productivity will grow at 1.0 percent, and columns 7 through 9 the trends under the very pessimistic assumption that future productivity will grow at 0.4 percent, the actual rate observed between 1973 and 1985. Under all three productivity assumptions it is apparent that after-tax compensation would ultimately grow more if the social security surplus were saved rather than used to pay for growing deficits in the non-OASDI government accounts. This result reflects the rise in national saving and the resulting increase in capital per worker and hence in productivity and real wages. Of course, workers pay a short-term penalty for the added national saving in the form of lower consumption. But the short-term sacrifice is eventually rewarded through higher after-tax earnings.[23]

The estimates in table 5-4 are also useful in deciding whether short-term consumption sacrifices are desirable. One's answer may depend, in part, on how fast one expects productivity to grow. If productivity grows rapidly, at 1.4 percent, net compensation would grow 12 percent faster between 1985 and 2020 under the increased saving option than under a pay-as-you-go tax formula.[24] Under the assumption that productivity grows at a rate of 1.0 percent, net compensation would grow nearly 20 percent faster by 2020 (79 percent

22. Gross compensation rates are identical in columns 1 and 2. Net compensation differs in the two columns only because of differences in the payroll tax rate implied by the two different taxing formulas.

23. The size of the short-term sacrifice and ultimate consumption gain is most clearly seen by comparing net compensation under a pay-as-you-go tax formula and under the increased saving alternative—that is, by comparing columns 1 and 3, 4 and 6, and 7 and 9 in table 5-4. The pay-as-you-go tax rate represents the lowest rate workers could pay in the short run that keeps the OASDI program solvent.

24. By 2020 net compensation grows 111 percent under the increased saving fiscal policy and tax schedule versus only 99 percent under the pay-as-you-go formula (columns 3 and 1, table 5-4).

versus 66 percent) if saving is increased by the additions to social security reserves than if it is not. And under the assumption of 0.4 percent growth, net compensation in 2020 would grow 41 percent faster (38 percent versus 27 percent) if national saving is increased by the amount of social security reserves.

These results indicate that a policy of increasing national saving is a kind of insurance against the possibility of slow growth in productivity. The slower is the anticipated growth in productivity arising from improvements in technology, the greater is the relative dependence of labor productivity on increases in the capital stock per worker. This is why a slowdown in productivity growth can have a profound effect on one's view of alternative mechanisms for financing social security. Under an optimistic assumption about future productivity, workers in 2020 will receive about twice the net compensation per hour received by workers today. Their compensation would be about 6 percent higher if a consumption sacrifice were made today in order to reduce the OASDI burden on those workers. But under the most pessimistic assumption, net compensation in 2020 will be only about a quarter above what it is today. Making a consumption sacrifice today and saving the social security surplus over the next generation would raise the after-tax compensation of those workers by an additional 11 percent.

The same kind of pattern is evident in the fortunes of future beneficiaries. Table 5-5 shows the trend in real, after-tax average benefits under the alternative assumptions about future fiscal policy and productivity growth.[25] After-tax benefits are calculated by subtracting the federal income tax payments levied on OASDI benefits. For each productivity assumption, the table shows benefit trends under the baseline fiscal policy and the policy that results in higher national saving. Real benefits rise faster if saving is increased because benefits are ultimately determined by past real wages, which in turn are raised by a fiscal policy involving greater government saving.

Once again, the relative importance of increasing saving by the

25. The average annual social security benefit grows more slowly than average compensation per hour under all three productivity assumptions. Future average benefits are scheduled to decline relative to average taxable wages because of the rise in the normal retirement age from sixty-five to sixty-seven. Under the II-B assumptions adopted in 1986, taxable wages are projected to fall relative to compensation as a result of the expected rise in fringe benefits. And annual compensation will grow more slowly than hourly compensation because of the projected drop in the length of the work week.

TABLE 5-5. **After-Tax Growth in the Real Average Benefits Paid by Social Security under Varying Assumptions about Productivity Growth and Fiscal Policy, Selected Years, 1986–2060**[a]

1985 = 100

Year	Productivity growth of 1.4 percent[b]		Productivity growth of 1.0 percent		Productivity growth of 0.4 percent	
	Baseline (1)	Increased saving (2)	Baseline (3)	Increased saving (4)	Baseline (5)	Increased saving (6)
1986	101	101	101	101	101	101
1990	101	101	101	101	101	101
2000	107	107	105	106	102	103
2010	113	116	107	110	99	103
2020	129	135	116	123	100	107
2030	144	153	124	133	100	108
2040	162	172	133	142	100	108
2050	185	194	144	152	100	107
2060	213	223	157	165	100	107

Source: Authors' calculations as explained in the text.

a. Average benefits are calculated as total OASDI benefits, adjusted for federal income tax withholdings returned to the OASDI trust fund, measured in constant dollars and divided by the total number of OASDI beneficiaries.

b. The assumed rate of growth in total factor productivity that underlies the II-B projections and the baseline projections of our model averages 1.4 percent annually.

social security surplus is greater the slower is the assumed rate of productivity growth. In fact, average social security benefits cease growing altogether under the most pessimistic productivity assumption unless the social security surplus is saved (table 5-5, columns 5 and 6). In such a case, improvements in future real benefits depend entirely on adopting a fiscal policy that raises national saving. Thus, for future beneficiaries as well as workers, the fiscal policy adopted over the next several decades can have major effects on the trend in living standards if productivity follows our pessimistic assumptions.

Reducing the Burden on Future Generations

The results presented in this chapter indicate that the costs of old-age, survivors, and disability pensions and of medicare hospital benefits will impose little burden on future generations of active workers, provided that steps are taken now to increase national saving. A policy of setting social security and medicare payroll taxes to keep each program in close actuarial balance will achieve this end, if fiscal policy is managed so that the resulting increase in reserves adds to national saving. If national saving is not increased, then these programs will impose significantly greater burdens on future generations than they do on current generations. Those burdens will be manageable if productivity growth recovers to the pre-1973 rate, but they will be very heavy if the improvement in general living standards continues at the recent dismal pace.

It is important to recognize that the elderly and disabled beneficiaries of social security pensions and medicare hospitalization benefits (part A) will also qualify for medicare physician benefits (part B), medicaid payments for long-term care, and any other health benefits that may be enacted in the future. Costs of these programs, like those analyzed here, will have to be met out of current production. Unless the nation increases saving enough to raise production by the costs of these programs, they will impose some burden on future generations of active members of the labor force.

The results presented here should not be interpreted as implying that saving is the principal determinant of economic growth. It is not. Growth depends on numerous factors, the most important of which are technological advance and the increased education and skills of workers.[26] Rather our findings indicate that burdens of programs for the aged and disabled will be sizable if nothing is done now to prepare for them, but that they can be offset by undertaking the kind of long-term planning traditionally practiced in the social security program, together with fiscal and monetary policies that will increase national saving.

If saving is increased now in anticipation of these costs, future generations need bear little burden from the withdrawal of production to provide OASDHI benefits for the elderly and disabled. Such saving can increase the U.S. national product sufficiently to cover essentially all of those costs. In estimating the impact of capital formation on future output we have followed a conservative strategy of not attributing to capital formation any power to increase the long-run rate of technological advance; capital contributes only its own marginal product.

We conclude that fears concerning the large burdens social security will impose on active workers are overblown. Such burdens will be substantial if future productivity growth is low or if nothing is done to anticipate them, but they can be avoided if action to increase

26. A recent accounting for past contributions to U.S. economic growth is provided in Edward F. Denison, *Trends in American Economic Growth, 1929–1982* (Brookings, 1985).

national saving is undertaken promptly. The fear that health benefits for the aged will impose onerous future burdens appears to have a better basis in fact. Much of that burden, however, arises from the inexorable rise in the price and use of medical care, not from the graying of the American population. To the extent that national saving is increased in anticipation of these rising costs, the future burden of medicare benefits also can be reduced.

The accumulation of social security and medicare reserves is one way by which such an increase could be achieved. But such methods as budget surpluses on other operations of the federal government or effective policies to increase private saving could be equally effective, if they could be identified and implemented.

Continuation of current federal deficits, which reduce national saving, carries a deferred cost in the form of reduced national income that will be most evident at the very time the baby-boom generation retires. Were the overall federal deficit to continue and to average 4 percent of gross national product, consumption (derived by the methods used in this chapter) would be reduced below our baseline values by 2.9 percent in 2030 and by 7.1 percent in 2060.

CHAPTER 6

Investment Policy

INCREASED national saving brought about by the accumulation of reserves in the social security fund can help future generations meet the costs of pension and hospital insurance benefits for a growing population of beneficiaries. But what will the investment of those social security reserves do to the economy? Will the accumulation of huge reserves disturb financial markets? For example, if the trust funds come to own most government debt, are relative returns on different types of assets likely to change? Would the Federal Reserve System be able to carry out open market operations if the trust funds came to own all Treasury debt? Can social security reserves be invested to yield higher returns, either for the social security system or for the economy as a whole, than would result from continued investment in special U.S. Treasury securities?

This chapter focuses on two distinct roles played by social security reserves—first as financial support for social security itself, and second as an element of overall fiscal policy that influences national saving and investment.

Financial Markets

Events in financial markets and social security financing will profoundly affect one another. Consider the impact that changing the assumptions about interest rates would have. The assumptions underlying the II-B actuarial projections in the 1986 report of the social security trustees imply that unless future tax rates are increased, the system would ultimately face a cumulative deficit that reaches 11.1 percent of net national product by 2060. In that projection, the real rate of interest on social security reserves is assumed to be a constant 2 percent.[1] Increasing the assumed rate of return to 3 percent over the seventy-five-year period converts this deficit into a surplus equal to 5 percent of NNP in 2060—a gain in the ultimate reserve position

1. *Economic Projections for OASDHI Cost and Income Estimates, 1986*, Actuarial Study 98 (Baltimore, Md.: Social Security Administration, 1987), p. 68.

amounting to 16 percent of NNP. A drop in the real rate of interest would produce equally dramatic opposite effects.

The critical role played by interest rates is new to social security. It has emerged because for the first time accumulated reserves will be several times as large as annual outlays, and interest earnings will represent a sizable fraction of the trust funds' total income. Yet nobody can reliably forecast interest rates.

Social Security and Hospital Insurance Financing and the Public Debt

The financing of old-age, survivors, disability, and hospital insurance (OASDHI) will influence financial markets by changing the composition of financial assets held by the public. Those effects do not appear in our baseline simulation because it stipulates that the overall budget deficit remains at 1.5 percent of GNP (the historical average), with fluctuations in the trust fund fully offset by changes in the balance on other government operations. Consequently, the publicly held debt— that is, the debt not held in the trust funds—would continue to grow annually by an amount equal to about 1.5 percent of GNP.[2] Since GNP grows faster than 1.5 percent per year, the ratio of the publicly held debt in our baseline projection to GNP falls from 0.44 in 1990 to 0.30 by 2060. This is well within the range of historical experience.

An alternative would be to hold the deficit exclusive of social security constant at 1.5 percent of GNP, but with currently legislated OASDI tax rates. In that case the OASDI surplus would be fully reflected in reduced Treasury borrowing from the private market. The fraction of Treasury debt held by the public would fall. The trust funds would acquire 98 percent of the Treasury debt by 2020, the year when the ratio of social security reserves to public debt attains its maximum. Subsequently the publicly held debt would again grow rapidly as the social security system began to sell off its Treasury holdings to finance benefit payments.

On the other hand, if tax rates were increased to maintain actuarial balance, as discussed in chapter 5, the OASDI trust funds would own all of the federal debt by 2010. At their peak, the funds' reserves would exceed the available public debt by an amount equivalent to 10 percent of GNP. The Treasury would not resume debt issues to the public until after 2040.[3]

2. The increment to the public debt is not precisely equal to the deficit in each year because of fluctuations in Treasury cash balances and seigniorage on coins.

3. The effect on the public debt would be even more pronounced if payroll taxes

Elimination of the market for government securities would raise concern about the functioning of financial markets. The market for Treasury bills is a major source of liquidity for American investors because both the outstanding stock and the daily volume of trade in most private securities are far smaller than are those of Treasury securities. The complete elimination of a Treasury debt market would also complicate the operation of monetary policy. However, the prospect that the trust funds will buy up all securities guaranteed as to principal and interest by the U.S. government is unlikely and certainly will not occur soon. Furthermore, the OASDHI trust funds could be authorized to invest in the sizable quantity of securities issued by federal agencies that are backed by government-guaranteed mortgages or other assets.

Interest Rates and the Composition of Debt

Economists divide into two camps on how a reduction in the publicly held federal debt might influence interest rates. According to those who accept the notion of segmented markets, investors have preferences for specific financial assets based on such attributes as marketability, risk of default, and maturity. If these preferences were strong, changes in the composition of assets would have pronounced effects on interest rates. According to this view, a drop in the the ratio of Treasury securities to other financial assets would widen the yield differential between relatively risky, private financial securities and relatively safe Treasury securities.

In contrast, advocates of the idea of integrated markets conclude that changes in the composition of assets have little effect on relative interest rates. According to this view, investors who hold mixed portfolios of low-risk Treasury securities and other, risky assets can nearly duplicate the characteristics of such portfolios by choosing a different mix of assets. According to this view, changes in the

---

for medicare hospital insurance were also increased to maintain close actuarial balance in the HI fund. The combined old-age and survivors insurance (OASI), disability insurance (DI), and hospital insurance (HI) trust funds would purchase all of the Treasury debt as early as 2006. By the year 2033, the government would hold debts of the general public amounting to 20 percent of NNP. After that year, however, the non-OASDHI deficit would exceed annual surpluses in the social security and medicare system. By 2056 the Treasury would once again begin issuing government debt to the public, and in 2060 this publicly held debt would amount to about 3 percent of NNP.

proportion of Treasury securities to total assets would have little effect on relative interest rates.

Current empirical research supports the integrated markets view more than the segmented markets view. Several studies have tried and failed to find any effect of changes in the relative quantities of short- and long-term assets on the pattern of interest rates on assets of varying maturities.[4] In addition, the composition of U.S. financial assets has varied widely since 1955 (figure 6-1). The share of Treasury issues in total financial assets fell from 42 percent in 1955 to 23 percent in 1986. Meanwhile, the proportion of mortgages rose from 22 percent in 1955 to 32 percent in 1986. Despite such large changes in the composition of assets, relative interest rates on federal government bonds, corporate bonds, mortgages, and state and local government securities fluctuated within a narrow band and displayed no trend relative to one another (figure 6-2).

Statistical analysis confirms a simple reading of the data. One study sought to determine whether changes in interest differentials could be traced to changes in the relative supply of various assets. Technical factors (such as the risk of early redemption) and business cycle conditions (represented by the unemployment rate) can explain the interest rate differentials among assets with an error of only 15 basis points. The relative quantities of securities were statistically insignificant.[5]

These results suggest that the OASDHI system could absorb a large fraction of outstanding Treasury debt without pushing down yields relative to interest rates on other securities. These estimates do not indicate whether reduction in the quantity of federal debt in the hands of the public below the historical range would affect relative interest rates.

---

4. See, for example, Franco Modigliani and Richard Sutch, "Innovations in Interest Rate Policy," *American Economic Review*, vol. 56 (May 1966, *Papers and Proceedings, 1966*), pp. 178–97; and Barry P. Bosworth, Andrew S. Carron, and Elisabeth H. Rhyne, *The Economics of Federal Credit Programs* (Brookings, 1987), pp. 177–204.

5. Based on an equation in Bosworth, Carron, and Rhyne, *Economics of Federal Credit Programs*, p. 195. The equation equates the effective yield on callable corporate new issues to the effective yield on twenty-year government bonds, the index of the probability of early redemption, the four-quarter change in the unemployment rate of married men, the two-year average of the interest rate differential between commercial paper and Treasury bills, and the current and lagged values of the share of corporate bonds in private-sector financial portfolios. The coefficients of the share of corporate bonds in private-sector financial portfolios were statistically insignificant.

FIGURE 6-1. **Composition of Financial Assets in the United States and Public Debt as a Percent of Gross National Product, 1955–86**

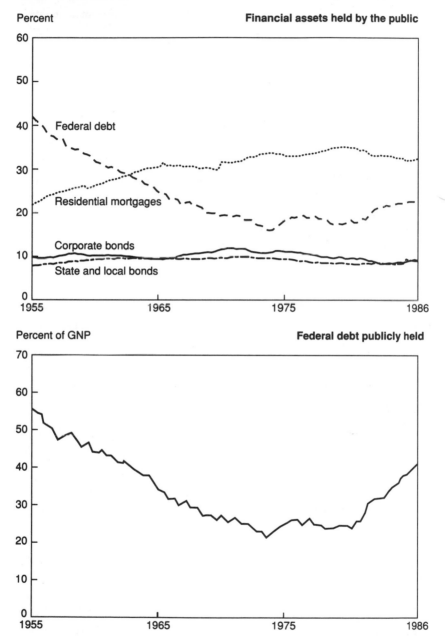

Source: Board of Governors of the Federal Reserve System, *Flow of Funds Accounts: Financial Assets and Liabilities*, various years; and authors' calculations. Total financial assets include items not shown separately.

FIGURE 6-2. **Relation of Rates on Private and Other Government Securities to Rate on Federal Government Bonds, 1955–86**

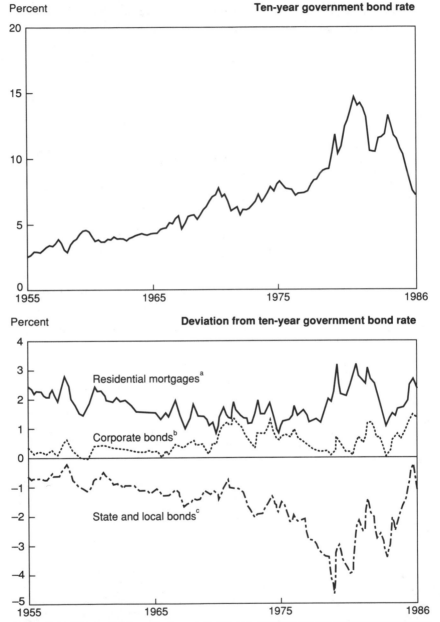

Percent   **Ten-year government bond rate**

Percent   **Deviation from ten-year government bond rate**

Source: *Federal Reserve Bulletin,* various issues, table 1.35; and unpublished data from the Board of Governors of the Federal Reserve System.
   a. Effective interest rate on conventional mortgages.
   b. Effective yield on new-issue deferred-call AA industrial bonds.
   c. Effective yield on new-issue municipal bonds.

Maintaining Liquidity

Legal requirements force some investors to hold part or all of their portfolios in Treasury securities. Reduction in the quantity of Treasury securities below that necessary to satisfy these legal demands would tend to drive up the price of those securities or, in other words, to drive down the interest rate on federal debt. This possibility should cause little concern, however, as such legal requirements could be modified at slight cost if the relative yields on various assets changed sharply.

A more important argument rests on the value of maintaining adequate financial liquidity. The market for short-term Treasury securities (bills) is an important source of liquidity for the U.S. financial system. Like money, such assets carry little or no risk of default or capital loss from interest rate fluctuations but have the advantage of paying interest. Because transactions in Treasury securities with a maturity of less than one year are so large—a daily average of $36 billion during 1986—individual investors need not worry that their actions will materially affect market rates of interest. Some liquidity needs met by the market for Treasury bills could be satisfied in the market for commercial paper or bankers' acceptances, but these markets are thinner and traders in such markets accept some slight risk of default.

The Federal Reserve also uses Treasury securities to carry out its open market operations. Gross purchases totaled $24 billion in 1986; gross sales amounted to $3 billion. In addition, the Federal Reserve entered repurchase agreements totaling $170 billion as part of its efforts to smooth out short-run monetary conditions.[6]

If the market for Treasury securities contracted gradually over a number of years, institutions could find new ways to meet needs now satisfied by the market for Treasury securities. They could, for example, increase their holdings of a combination of money and private securities. The Federal Reserve could conduct open market operations with such securities as those of government-sponsored agencies, bankers' acceptances, or foreign exchange.

The current system, however, is highly efficient because Treasury bills are so widely accepted and traded. It would be convenient to retain this market. The issue will become important only if the federal

6. Board of Governors of the Federal Reserve System, *Federal Reserve Bulletin*, vol. 73 (June 1987), pp. A9, A31.

government becomes a huge net saver by running surpluses large enough to buy up almost all of the outstanding federal debt. In that event, the OASDHI system would have to invest in other assets than it now does.

Investing Social Security Reserves

Social security reserves are currently invested in special issues of the U.S. Treasury that are not publicly traded.[7] The interest rate paid on new issues by law is the average rate on currently outstanding U.S. government debt with a maturity of four years or more. The managing trustee of the OASDHI trust funds (the secretary of the treasury) can resell these securities to the Treasury at par at any time. This option makes these securities as liquid as cash. In practice, the managing trustee has not used this privilege to redeem old, low-interest debt for new, high-interest debt when fluctuations in interest rates made such a strategy profitable. Nevertheless, this provision has spared the social security system the need to sell low-interest securities at a loss on the open market when deficits forced asset sales.[8] Instead, the trustee follows a simple last-in-first-out (LIFO) policy when assets must be sold.

All or part of social security reserves could be invested in other assets. The principal alternatives are publicly traded Treasury securities or issues of the government-sponsored agencies that are guaranteed as to principal and interest, securities issued by government-sponsored agencies that are not guaranteed, and private securities and real estate. Current law permits the first of these alternatives

7. In previous years, the trust funds have held some publicly traded Treasury issues and federally sponsored agency obligations. The last such holdings in the old-age and survivors insurance trust fund were liquidated in 1982. The hospital insurance trust fund held some obligations of federally sponsored agencies in May 1988. Trust fund managers invest revenues not required for current operations in short-term securities that mature on the succeeding June 30th. The balance at that date is invested in securities maturing from one to fifteen years in the future. Purchases of each maturity are set so that the social security portfolio will consist of equal holdings in each maturity. Thus, the average maturity of the social security portfolio is close to seven and one-half years.

8. If the opportunity had arisen, this option would also have prevented the managing trustee from redeeming high-interest securities at a premium when low interest rates coincided with forced redemptions. Such opportunities were rare as high interest rates have coincided with periods when social security experienced unplanned deficits.

and a limited version of the second; the third would require enabling legislation.[9] All three types of assets are currently included in the portfolios of private pension funds.

The trust fund manager might wish to shift investment policy to reduce the possibility that successive Congresses and presidents will use social security reserves to pay for government consumption, to increase the rate of return earned on social security reserves, or to try to increase overall economic output. The first objective is important if the reserve is to reduce the future burden of social security benefits. An increase in the earnings rate on social security reserves that averaged 1.00 percentage point over the full seventy-five years would effectively substitute for an increase of 0.43 percentage point in the payroll tax rate.[10] And some people have argued that overall economic output could be increased if the reserves were used to finance specific sectors of the economy that capital markets erroneously judged to have poor prospects.

Marketed Government-Guaranteed Securities

The yield on bonds with distant maturities typically exceeds the yield on bonds of similar risk with shorter maturities. Standard theory suggests that the yield on long-term securities is an average of rates of return on short-term securities expected over the life of the long-term asset, plus a premium to compensate for the illiquidity of long-term assets.

The surpluses projected for the social security system over the next quarter century are so huge (and will be even larger if taxes follow the pattern indicated in chapter 3) that even if the projections are overoptimistic, large surpluses are almost certain to materialize. Thus, the trust funds can anticipate holding until maturity most of the portfolio they will acquire in the next few years, even if maturities stretch out to thirty years or more. Accordingly, it might seem attractive to invest social security reserves in assets with long maturities in order to capture the maximum bond yields. Most of the $25.5 billion of special Treasury issues in the social security portfolio on September 30, 1987, that were not in the portfolio one year earlier

9. *1988 Annual Report of the Board of Trustees of the Federal Old-Age and Survivors Insurance and Disability Insurance [OASDI] Trust Funds* (Baltimore, Md.: Social Security Administration, 1988), pp. 14–15.

10. In both cases, the combined old-age, survivors, and disability insurance trust funds would contain the same balance at the end of the projection period in 2060.

yielded 8.80 percent. The average yield during September 1987 on thirty-year Treasury securities was 9.59 percent.[11] While differentials of this size do not exist every year, the question of why they should not be taken when available certainly deserves consideration.

A strategy of investing in bonds with very long maturities suffers from serious disadvantages, however. Investment of the social security portfolio in long-term marketed assets would carry significant risks, some arising from the possible need to redeem securities before maturity when interest rates were above the coupon rate and some from the nature of the promise to pay social security benefits. Redemption before maturity when interest rates were above coupon rates would expose the trust funds to capital losses.

A more subtle problem concerns the nature of social security benefit obligations. Newly awarded old-age, survivors, and disability benefits are indexed according to changes in nominal wages. A jump in the rate of inflation that is reflected in money wages permanently increases benefit obligations. The longer the maturity of the social security portfolio, the more slowly the rate of return earned on that portfolio will respond to the higher interest rates normally associated with inflation. Thus, a bout of unanticipated inflation would force Congress to increase payroll taxes more than would be necessary if the portfolio turned over relatively quickly so that the benefit of higher returns could be quickly captured. To be sure, inflation might be unexpectedly low, creating windfall gains for the social security system that would be larger the longer the average maturity of the social security portfolio.[12]

The National Commission on Social Security Reform (chaired by Alan Greenspan) recommended that the trust funds invest in special assets that would pay an interest rate adjusted monthly to equal the average rate of interest on outstanding Treasury securities with a maturity of four years or more.[13] Both the House and the Senate included this provision in bills passed during 1983, but the conference

11. *1988 OASDI Annual Report*, pp. 22–23; and Board of Governors of the Federal Reserve System, *Federal Reserve Bulletin*, vol. 74 (January 1988), p. A24.

12. A forced tax increase has some economic advantage if inflation arises from excess demand. But a tax increase would be economically perverse if the inflation, like that of the 1970s and early 1980s, were triggered by an import price shock that was associated with a weak domestic economy.

13. *Report of the National Commission on Social Security Reform* (GPO, January 1983), pp. 2-20, 2-21.

committee omitted it from the final bill amending the Social Security Act.

The social security system can increase interest earnings, but only with added risk from variations in interest rates. The current social security portfolio—with maturities evenly spread over fifteen years, averaging seven and one-half years—seems to us a reasonable compromise between the goals of maximizing returns and minimizing risk.

Shifting to longer-term investments would not in any way insulate social security reserves from use as an offset to government spending on other accounts, since the purchase of long-term bonds would have the same effect on the sale of Treasury debt to the public as does the issuance of special issues. Such a change in social security investment policy would have little effect on private investment or economic growth.

Securities of Government-Sponsored Agencies

Government-sponsored enterprises carry out a large volume of credit activities. The Federal Home Loan Banks (FHLBs), for example, borrow directly from the public and lend the proceeds to member savings and loan associations. The bonds issued by the FHLBs typically bear a rate of interest roughly 0.5 percentage point higher than do Treasury securities of the same maturity. The Federal National Mortgage Association (FNMA) buys mortgages guaranteed by the Veterans Administration and the Federal Housing Administration with proceeds from bonds sold to the public.[14] The Government National Mortgage Association (GNMA) and the Federal Home Loan Mortgage Corporation, a subsidiary of the FHLB system, undertake similar activities.[15] In addition, these agencies sell securities not guaranteed by the federal government that are backed by pools of mortgage loans, some of which are government guaranteed.[16] The

14. It also acts as a facilitator and guarantor for mortgage-backed securities. It sells shares in a pool of mortgages to private investors who receive the principal and interest payments of the underlying mortgages. Ownership of a share in the pool is less risky than purchase of an individual mortgage. FNMA guarantees the timely payment of interest and the ultimate repayment of principal.

15. The GNMA is included in the budget as part of the Department of Housing and Urban Development.

16. These activities are described in Bosworth, Carron, and Rhyne, *Economics of Federal Credit Programs*.

TABLE 6-1. **New and Outstanding Debt of Government-Sponsored Enterprises, 1987**
Billions of dollars

Enterprise	Total outstanding debt	Net change during 1987
Student Loan Marketing Association	21.3	5.8
Federal National Mortgage Association	223.2	45.2
Farm Credit Banks	54.4	−9.6
Federal Home Loan Bank System	105.6	17.5
Federal Home Loan Mortgage Corporation	225.4	65.6
Gross borrowing	629.9	124.4
Total borrowing[a]	624.1	124.8

Source: *Special Analyses: Budget of the United States Government, Fiscal Year 1989*, pp. F-89 and F-90.
a. Excludes funds borrowed from federal sources.

Student Loan Marketing Association (SLMA) does for guaranteed student loans what FNMA formerly did for home mortgages. It sells bonds to the public and uses the proceeds to buy loans that banks have made to students under the Guaranteed Student Loan Program. Its bonds are effectively as secure as Treasury issues, because SLMA bonds are backed by a portfolio of government-guaranteed securities.

These credit operations involve very large financial flows (table 6-1). And in all cases these assets yield more than do Treasury securities of the same maturities. Such investments would have an advantage over the special issues in which reserves are now invested because the higher yields would improve the financial standing of the social security trust funds. We see no persuasive argument based on the riskiness of such assets against the investment of social security reserves in such assets rather than publicly marketed Treasury securities.[17] It is important to recognize, however, that any increase in yields earned by the social security system is largely a kind of financial musical chairs. Private investors would hold the lower-yield, lower-risk Treasury securities previously held by social security.

If private investors tried to restore the balance between risk and yield that they previously enjoyed, real economic effects could result. For example, some private investors might shift to higher-yield securities issued by foreign governments or businesses to achieve their desired mix of risk and return. Such a shift would affect

17. The special issues in which trust funds are now invested, which can be redeemed on demand at par, have a major advantage over all marketed securities, which can be sold before maturity only at the prevailing market price.

international capital flows, exchange rates, and international trade. Because securities of federal agencies are close substitutes for treasuries, the effects on international capital flows may be trivial.

Investment of social security reserves in the assets of credit agencies might help insulate these reserves from other parts of the budget by differentiating the operations of the trust funds from the routine financing of government debt. Congress has already removed social security from the budget and has stipulated that medicare hospital insurance be removed in 1993. To be sure, Congress undermined in one paragraph its intent declared in another by including social security surpluses as offsets against deficits generated by other federal activities for purposes of meeting deficit reduction targets defined in the Balanced Budget Act of 1985. However, operations of many government-sponsored enterprises are currently not included in the budget, and their financial activities are not regarded as part of the federal budget. Encouraging social security to invest in assets of such enterprises would strengthen the case for excluding these funds from politically salient measures of the federal deficit.[18]

Currently, the outstanding borrowings of government-sponsored enterprises slightly exceed $600 billion or an amount equal to 14 percent of GNP.[19] If this debt continues to expand in line with GNP, it would provide a potential source of assets for social security that, together with Treasury debt, would exceed the size of the reserve buildup at its peak. Thus, the expansion of the social security portfolio to include these securities is one means by which the elimination of an active market in Treasury securities, sufficient to meet private liquidity needs and the operation of monetary policy, could be avoided.

Private Securities

Social security reserves could be invested directly in private stocks or bonds either to provide resources to sectors of the economy deemed worthy of special support or to earn an increased rate of return for the trust funds. Whether or not the federal government should try to manage the allocation of capital among competing industries is a question that transcends the issue of how social security reserves ought to be invested.

18. Chapter 7 considers the question of how the OASDHI programs should be handled in government budgeting.

19. *Special Analyses: Budget of the United States Government, Fiscal Year 1989,* p. F90.

The reserves could be invested in the private economy in ways that precluded active management by federal officials. For example, a portion of social security reserves, much like private pension funds, could be invested broadly across a large number of private securities— the Standard and Poor's index of five hundred leading stocks or the Wilshire 5000 index—with no intent to affect the allocation of capital. If this course were followed, social security reserves would be subject to the wide fluctuations in asset values characteristic of private securities.

This increase in risk might be worth bearing if such an investment strategy could be shown to increase the efficiency of investment. If total saving is unaffected, however, no such benefit should be expected, as the following example indicates. Suppose that total saving in the economy is 700, consisting of a government deficit of 100 and 800 in private saving; that the total government deficit consists of a deficit apart from social security of 300 and a social security surplus of 200. Because the government is borrowing 100, only 700 out of private saving will be available for private investment. Alternatively, if social security reserves were invested entirely in private securities, so that the government was forced to borrow 300 from private lenders, the amount available to private investors would be unchanged even though the source of their financing would change. Given these values, social security investment policy will affect borrowing in the following way:

	Social security reserves invested in	
	Treasury securities	*Private securities*
Treasury borrowing	300	300
From social security	200	0
From all other sources	100	300
Private borrowing	700	700
From social security	0	200
From all other sources	700	500

As this example indicates, however, whether social security invests directly in Treasury securities or in private securities has no first-order effect on the amount of private investment.

How social security invests its reserves might influence the portfolios that private wealth holders elect to hold, and these decisions would generate secondary economic effects. Private investors who prefer riskier, higher-yielding portfolios than they would hold if they invested in Treasury securities might be induced to increase holdings of foreign securities. Such a shift in preferences would cause a short-run decline in the exchange value of the U.S. dollar and a short-run increase in net exports. Eventually, the increased holdings of foreign assets will generate a flow of income back to the United States, increasing the exchange rate and imports in the long run.

These shifts in asset ownership would not materially change the composition of U.S. investment in real capital, output, or economic growth. Whether the investment of social security reserves in private assets is desirable, like the question of whether social security should increase the maturity of its bond portfolio, hinges on whether the added income to the trust funds justifies the increased risk of the portfolio that it holds.

A policy of investing social security reserves in private securities would force the government either to make difficult decisions about how to exercise the right to vote in corporate elections that equity ownership confers or to select a form of investment that obviates the need to make these choices. How to vote shares raises vexing questions for pension funds, especially in the case of proposed takeovers.[20] The trust funds could avoid such questions by buying shares of mutual funds, although as a large if not dominant investor, the managing trustee of the OASDHI funds would still have considerable potential power over corporate policy.

The social security reserves act both as a financial cushion for the social security system and as an instrument of fiscal policy that influences national saving. Investment of reserves in riskier assets than the special issues would increase interest income and somewhat reduce the payroll tax rates necessary to keep the system in close actuarial balance. In this sense, investment in riskier assets would reduce the apparent cost of providing benefits to workers.

The appearance is illusory. The cost of these programs depends on the level of benefits and on productive capacity of the nation at the time the benefits are paid. How social security reserves are invested has little to do with the amount or composition of national investment.

20. See U.S. General Accounting Office, *Pension Plans and Corporate Takeovers*, GAO/HRD-88-58 (Washington, D.C., March 1988).

For this reason, investment policy has little bearing on economic growth.

Whether the selection of assets for the social security portfolio affects the likelihood that other government policies allow social security surpluses to increase government saving is a matter of political judgment, not science. We think that a policy of investing part of social security reserves in assets of government-sponsored enterprises will help insulate the reserves from being used to pay for current government activities. It will certainly increase the yield that can be reasonably anticipated on the social security portfolio. A policy of investing in the private sector would raise a host of issues—whether the federal government would or should use these investments to influence private investment and management—that have little to do with the management of social security and would pointlessly expose social security reserves to economic and political risks.

On balance, we think that it would be unwise to invest social security reserves directly in private securities and debt instruments. This decision should certainly not be influenced by the wholly erroneous view that failure to invest directly in private assets means that additions to social security reserves will not increase private investment. Whether social security surpluses add to private investment hinges entirely on whether they add to national saving, not on the particular assets in which they are invested.

Summary

The United States has now embarked on a policy of building social security reserves. These reserves are economically important primarily because they can increase national saving. Such savings can help increase U.S. economic growth. Whether the resulting social security reserves are invested in Treasury debt or other securities will have small secondary economic effects. Which assets are purchased with social security reserves will have little effect on the composition of real investment and hence on economic growth. This decision can influence the rate of return earned and the risk associated with the social security portfolio. Furthermore, the choice of assets may have some influence on the willingness of successive Congresses and presidents not to use social security reserves to offset deficits on other government operations.

CHAPTER 7

Policy Options

SOCIAL SECURITY and medicare hospital insurance combine all the characteristics needed to provoke intense public debate. They constitute the principal source of income for most retirees and the promised foundation of the future retirement income of more than 90 percent of active workers and their families. The payroll taxes collected for old-age, survivors, disability, and hospital insurance (OASDHI) supply more than one-third of federal revenues and represent the largest tax burden borne by most taxpayers. The program rules are technically complex. They entail long-term promises stretching into the indefinite future that depend on the willingness of successive generations of voters to pay the taxes necessary to redeem these promises, and they require workers to have trust that obligations of vital personal importance will be met. Recently, the programs have experienced serious financial crises that aroused concern among beneficiaries about the sustainability of current benefits and among workers about the likelihood that they will ultimately receive the benefits promised under current law.

As a result of the 1977 and 1983 amendments to the Social Security Act, social security reserves are projected to increase dramatically. Part of this increase is necessary to reestablish an adequate contingency reserve, a cushion of funds sufficient to prevent forced tax increases because of an unexpected fall of revenues or rise in expenditures during recessions. Opinions differ on how large reserves should be to meet contingencies.[1] But, under any reasonable definition, the

1. A reserve equal to roughly one year of benefit payments is sufficient to allow benefits to be paid through a recession such as that experienced in 1973–74 without a tax increase if revenues slightly exceeded benefits at the start of the recession. A larger reserve, equal perhaps to one and one-half or two years of benefit payments, would be necessary if one serious recession were followed by another. Under current law, the start-of-year reserves for the old-age, survivors, and disability program are projected to equal annual expenditures in 1992 and twice annual expenditures in 1997. Reserves for hospital insurance currently exceed annual expenditures but are not projected to reach one and one-half times annual expenditures. *1988 Annual Report of the Board of Trustees of the Federal Old-Age and Survivors Insurance and Disability Insurance [OASDI] Trust Funds* (Baltimore, Md.: Social Security Administration, 1988), p. 83.

reserves projected under current law vastly exceed the amounts required to deal with contingencies. They can be justified only as part of an effort to increase incomes of future workers as an offset to the added cost of these programs.

This book examines the economic effects of accumulating such reserves and of increasing saving by a corresponding amount. The accumulation of large OASDHI reserves raises a number of questions involving both politics and economics that this chapter addresses before summarizing the major lessons of our analysis.

Two issues have arisen in response to the projected increases in costs of OASDHI and the accumulation of large surpluses. First, some analysts and a few members of Congress have proposed privatizing social security by replacing the public system with private pensions. American workers would be allowed or required to replace part or all of the OASDHI benefits to which they would become entitled under current law with private retirement accounts or health benefits. Second, although social security has been removed from the unified budget and hospital insurance will be removed in 1993 under current law, both remain within the deficit reduction targets set by the Balanced Budget Act of 1985. This ambiguous situation leaves unsettled whether debate about budget and economic policy will be facilitated by inclusion or exclusion of the social security and medicare programs from the official unified budget and from budget targets.

Privatization

Because people are myopic about the risks of disability and cost of retirement, there is a widely perceived need to compel workers to save for poor health and old age.[2] Of course, this goal need not be achieved through a public pension program like social security. Workers might simply be required to purchase old-age and disability insurance under some kind of private arrangement, such as a mandatory employer-provided pension plan. When social security was enacted in 1935, however, such private plans were rare. Many industrial and trade union plans had collapsed in the Great Depression,

2. Not all observers agree that compulsory saving for old age is desirable, regarding it instead as an unwarranted intrusion on human freedom. See, for example, Milton Friedman, *Capitalism and Freedom* (University of Chicago Press, 1962), pp. 187–89. The political popularity of social security suggests that the dissenting opinion is held by a small minority.

leaving covered workers without a dependable source of income in old age. Given these circumstances, it is hardly surprising that a public pension program, backed by the taxing authority of the state, was found preferable to the private alternative.

Private plans are much more common and appear more plausible as alternatives to social security and medicare in the 1980s than they did in the 1930s. Yet the social insurance programs continue to enjoy enormous popularity. They possess unique advantages that set them apart from privately funded alternatives. Based on experience over the past half century, social security and medicare seem much more secure than privately financed retirement benefits. Social security is not affected by financial market fluctuations, and benefits under the program have never been in jeopardy because of competitive losses suffered by individual companies, industries, or regions. Nor have benefits been substantially eroded by inflation. Even before they were legally indexed to the consumer price index in 1972, they were informally linked to prices by frequent amendments to the Social Security Act. Protection against inflation can be provided by a public pension program because of the government's authority to tax earnings, but such protection is impossible to obtain under a private plan.

Since its inception social security has served broader social aims, redistributing income from high- to low-wage workers and their dependents. Medicare hospital insurance accomplishes the same goal, because contributions to the program are determined by earnings but benefits depend on medical need. It is this redistributive objective that necessitates universal coverage and that, at the same time, leads to the desire of some workers to opt out of the programs.

The social security and medicare programs are only part of an overall system of publicly and privately supported benefits for the elderly and disabled. This system includes means-tested benefits for low-income households, such as supplemental security income, food stamps, and medicaid. And it includes private pension and disability programs, as well as private savings.

Some commentators have urged that the balance among these three elements be changed, by gradually reducing or eliminating the role played by social security and increasing reliance on means-tested programs and private pensions.[3] While current retirees and workers

3. Milton and Rose Friedman, *Free to Choose: A Personal Statement* (Harcourt Brace Jovanovich, 1980), pp. 123–24; and Peter J. Ferrara, "Social Security and the

soon to retire would continue to rely on social security, and the payroll or other taxes necessary to pay for these benefits would be retained, younger workers would be allowed or required to contribute to private pensions or to individual retirement accounts. In return, they would receive tax credits based on deposits in these private-sector savings vehicles and be compelled to forgo a part of the social security benefits to which they would otherwise eventually become entitled.

The economic case for privatization rests on the arguments that privatization will increase national saving and that retirement saving will be invested more efficiently than it now is, thus reducing the burden of future retirement benefits. But privatization raises important political questions. Can private plans offer the secure, inflation-proof benefits now offered under social security and medicare? Can alternative plans achieve the redistributional goals attained by these two programs? Social security benefits spare many low-income workers the need to apply for welfare or other income-tested assistance. Individual private pensions always return benefits based on amounts workers or their employers paid in.

Shifting to private savings accounts would eliminate or reduce the possibility of paying extra benefits to workers whose earnings have been low or to survivors and dependents in large families, and it would increase the number of applicants for welfare or other income-tested benefits. Such a course would pose an unattractive dilemma. Either it would necessitate a reduction or elimination of assistance to low-income households or it would require an increase in the number of elderly, survivors, and disabled who must apply for income- or means-tested payments.

In the short run, privatization cannot increase national saving, unless benefits to current retirees and workers on the verge of retirement are reduced or taxes on active workers are increased. Advocates of privatization typically do not favor either course. If social security benefits to current retirees are sustained and taxes continue to be collected to pay for them, the plan causes no immediate change in public spending or revenues. Any added saving in the alternative pension plan would be matched by increased deficits (or reduced surpluses) in the government budget arising from the tax credits. To

Super IRA: A Populist Proposal," in Peter J. Ferrara, ed., *Social Security: Prospects for Real Reform* (Washington, D.C.: Cato Institute, 1985), pp. 193–220.

be sure, taxes could be increased to offset the revenue loss from tax credits paid to workers who elect to leave social security; but this fact simply underscores the positive effect any tax increase has on national saving.

Over the long run, privatizing OASDI would raise national saving only to the extent that it leads to the accumulation of increased pension reserves or to smaller deficits on other government programs. If private pensions invest in riskier assets and generate correspondingly higher rates of return than OASDHI reserves earn, some secondary economic effects would follow similar to those resulting from a policy of investing OASDHI reserves in risky assets (which is analyzed in chapter 6).

A policy of building up retirement fund reserves can add to national saving, but whether such reserves are accumulated through OASDHI or through private pensions will not affect the capacity of such reserves to support increased investment. While privatization may reduce the risk that the reserve is used to finance current consumption, it causes side effects that we regard as objectionable—curtailing assistance to some workers and forcing some families onto welfare.

Advocates of privatization also claim that it will cut pension costs. Private pension plans will cost workers and their employers less than does social security, because, it is alleged, private plans could invest in riskier, higher-yielding assets than does social security.[4]

Privatization, like a shift in social security investment policy, would change the distribution of assets and of asset income between social security and private asset holders. If private pension funds invested added reserves as they invest those they now hold, privatization would increase the demand for assets that are riskier than government debt.[5] Private investors other than pension funds would find that the yields on private assets would fall and they would tend to look for higher-yielding securities, some of which would be found abroad. The economic effects of increasing the holdings of risky assets in

4. Of course, social security reserves could be invested in similar assets. As noted in chapter 6, such a policy would reduce the apparent cost of the social security system; a given set of benefits could be supported with reduced payroll taxes. But it would not by itself change either the size of social security benefits or national output and, hence, would not change the real cost of the program.

5. It is partly for this reason that retirement benefits provided by private plans are riskier than the benefits payable by social security. In addition, of course, it is not possible for private plans to invest in assets that are completely protected against unanticipated inflation.

private pension portfolios would be similar to those of investing OASDHI reserves in assets other than Treasury debt.

Savers will always earn a rate of return characteristic of the particular financial assets in which they invest. The return will be relatively low if the funds are invested in government securities, higher if they are invested in securities of government-sponsored agencies, and higher still if they are invested in private securities. But the yield to the economy arises not from a return paid to owners of particular legal certificates, but from the additional real goods and services produced because American workers have more capital goods with which to work or because American investors have larger claims on foreign assets.

In short, the move to privatize social security, like many other measures, might facilitate an increase in national saving; but so too would a change in fiscal policy that permits future social security surpluses to be reflected in smaller federal deficits or larger federal surpluses. Privatization would not change the physical assets in which national saving is invested. For that reason, the policy should be viewed primarily in political terms. It is a device that would eliminate the social security link between pension-type benefits and assistance to workers with lower-than-average earnings or larger-than-average families. It would thereby either increase the number of elderly and disabled persons who would require recourse to welfare or reduce the financial assistance provided to such workers.

Budget Accounting

The economic effects of using OASDHI surpluses to increase national saving will be the same whether or not social security and medicare expenditures and revenues are added to other expenditures and revenues in compiling the federal budget. The direct effects of the federal budget depend exclusively on federal spending and revenues, not on how accountants categorize them.[6] Whether these programs are included in or excluded from the budget is therefore of no direct economic significance whatsoever.

Budget accounting, however, may have considerable effects on public perceptions of the size of the federal deficit. If accounting

6. The budget may have numerous indirect effects on private saving through such channels as tax policy, direct loans, loan guarantees, and other channels that may change the level or composition of private spending.

procedures influence debate and policy on the size of the federal deficit (see table 1-3), these perceptions can have significant indirect economic effects (as discussed in chapter 5).

Budget accountants have treated social security and medicare hospital benefits in different ways at different times. Until fiscal 1969, social security and medicare were excluded from the administrative budget, the accounts on which most public attention focused. Starting in fiscal 1969, public debate shifted to the unified budget, which included both social security and medicare. The social security amendments of 1983 provided that social security and medicare would be removed from the unified budget in fiscal 1993. Although 1986 legislation stipulated that social security should be removed from the budget in fiscal 1986 and reaffirmed the later removal of medicare, the deficit reduction targets were set to include the OASDHI surpluses.

Whether one thinks that the social security and medicare programs should be included in or excluded from the official budget hinges on how one answers three questions. Should the federal fiscal policy be used to increase long-run national saving? Will the exclusion of the OASDHI programs over the long run lead to smaller or larger overall budget deficits? Will exclusion of these programs inhibit or complicate the formulation of short-run fiscal policy?

Unfortunately, no definitive answer exists to any of these questions. We have shown that increases in national saving equal to the buildup of reserves in the old-age, survivors, and disability funds are sufficient to relieve future generations of workers of all or most of the burden from the added costs of pension benefits. Whether such an increase in saving is socially or economically desirable hinges on value judgments about whether the gains in future consumption are sufficient to compensate for the losses from current reductions in consumption. On balance, we think that the case for increasing U.S. national saving is strong and that the future costs of social security and medicare provide both the occasion and the means for adding to national saving. The importance of such an increase in saving grows the less rapid technological growth turns out to be (for reasons set forth in chapter 5).

Whether the exclusion of OASDHI programs will lead to larger deficits (or smaller surpluses) hinges on whether the exclusion will induce more or less vigorous efforts to reduce the deficit. It also hinges on whether the undoubted temptation of elected officials to use accumulated OASDHI reserves to underwrite expenditures for which tax revenues seem insufficient will be reduced or intensified by exclusion of these programs from the budget.

Since the effect of the budget on current economic activity depends on all government spending and revenues, measures of the budget that include OASDHI are probably better guides to the short-run effects of the federal budget on current economic activity. Such considerations argue for defining the budget deficit inclusive of the OASDHI programs. However, because the size of the OASDHI trust fund surplus typically changes little from year to year, its inclusion in or exclusion from measures of the deficit will have little effect on fiscal policy since decisions on fiscal policy typically are based on changes in the size of the overall deficit.

We think that the chances of persuading the public of the desirability of paying currently for current government services and accumulating reserves for future obligations, such as OASDHI benefits, will be enhanced by excluding the OASDI and HI programs from the budget. This view implies that the long-run government deficit will be smaller or the surplus will be larger—and, hence, that national saving will be higher—if the OASDI and HI programs are kept out of the budget and are excluded in the future from deficit reduction targets. Such a course means that budget totals will not accurately indicate the full economic consequences of all government spending and revenues. However, officials responsible for setting budget and monetary policy will find it easy to add the relevant numbers. It would be far more difficult for the general public and their elected officials to remember that a surplus of payroll taxes over current OASDHI benefits is intended to help meet future benefit obligations if these surpluses appear in official budget numbers only as offsets to current deficits in other government operations.

Policy Recommendations

According to official projections, the proportion of net national product absorbed by social security will rise from 5.4 percent in 1986 to about 7 percent before declining gradually by about 0.5 percentage point. Over the same period, the combined cost of social security and medicare hospital insurance will rise from 6.7 percent to over 10 percent of net national product. Most of this increase will be concentrated in the three decades starting in 2005. It reflects a projected rise in the ratio of beneficiaries to active workers and in the ratio of per capita hospital costs to per capita earnings.

An increase in the proportion of national product flowing to OASDHI beneficiaries means that a smaller proportion will be available for consumption by the rest of the population or for investment at home or abroad. In this book we have explored the impact on consumption of the rest of the population that results from the increase in the cost of OASDHI, and how increases in national saving might offset those costs. The increases in national saving that we examine are related to the projected OASDI and HI annual surpluses.

Our first major conclusion is that whether these surpluses are large or small will matter little economically if they do not cause the overall federal deficit to fall (or a possible future surplus to rise). Only by increasing national saving through increases in government saving can the OASDHI surpluses affect economic growth.

Actual surpluses are likely to exceed those foreseen in the official projections. Even if all of the economic and demographic assumptions underlying official projections are exactly realized, it is not possible to retain the current benefit formula and payroll tax rates and to maintain close actuarial balance. *We conclude that if the current benefit formula is retained and if Congress imposes level tax increases to keep social security in close actuarial balance, increases in payroll taxes totaling about 2.4 percentage points will be necessary over the next seventy-five years to pay for social security. Payroll tax increases totaling 6.9 percentage points will be necessary to pay for both social security and medicare hospital insurance.*

If taxes are increased in this manner (or if benefits are cut to sustain close actuarial balance), the OASDHI trust funds will be considerably larger than those indicated in the official trust fund projections. Official projections indicate that the social security trust funds will first rise, reaching a maximum around 2030, and then fall until they are exhausted around 2050.[7] If the tax increases necessary to keep social security in close actuarial balance are enacted, the trust funds will never be exhausted. Although the trust funds will decline relative to national income, they will continue growing in absolute size. Our projections indicate that by 2060 social security reserves will equal 25 percent of net national product; in contrast, the official projections indicate a deficit of 11 percent of net national product.

7. *1988 OASDI Annual Report*, p. 141.

It is of course possible that Congress might elect not to raise taxes or to raise them by a smaller amount. In either case, it would have to either cut benefits or adopt a different standard for determining the adequacy of social security financing.

It might choose not to raise taxes or to cut benefits sufficiently to maintain actuarial balance over a period as lengthy as seventy-five years. Such a course might have considerable political appeal. The 1988 actuarial projections indicate that social security revenues will exceed expenditures by 2.15 percent of payroll over the twenty-five years ending in 2012 and by 0.35 percent of payroll over the fifty years ending in 2037.[8] If Congress relaxed its definition of close actuarial balance by using a shorter projection period for social security than seventy-five years or by allowing a shortfall of 10–15 percent of projected costs before declaring imbalance, the signal for tax increases or benefit cuts would be deferred for decades.

An alternative actuarial standard would impose tighter standards for actuarial balance of revenues and expenditures projected twenty-five years into the future than for longer periods. For example, social security funds might be judged to be in close actuarial balance if revenues projected over twenty-five years are not less than, say, 3 percent less than projected expenditures, 6 percent over fifty years, and 10 percent over seventy-five years. Such an approach would give explicit meaning to the rapidly increasing uncertainty as one looks farther into the future.

It is also essential to recognize that Congress could retain the current structure and level of OASDHI benefits, retain the current definition of close actuarial balance, and select a tax schedule that would not generate more than a contingency reserve. Such a policy would entail reductions in payroll taxes below those in current law for the next two or three decades, but it would require taxes in later years well above those in current law.

Pursuing such a course would abandon attempts to use trust fund surpluses to add to national saving and surrender the opportunity to use such savings to increase the capital stock and add to future production. This comment follows from our next major conclusion. *If fiscal policy is managed so that additions to the OASDHI trust funds add to national saving, the resulting increase in national consumption will exceed the increased costs of social security benefits and come*

8. Ibid., p. 72.

close to offsetting the increased costs of OASDHI benefits from a growing population of beneficiaries and rising hospital costs. In short, the rising costs of social security and medicare hospital benefits represent a significant cost for future generations. To the extent that this cost is a source of concern, our simulations indicate that a straightforward device exists for offsetting it. If the federal government adheres to the principle that social security should be kept in close actuarial balance over the succeeding seventy-five years and that medicare hospital insurance should be brought into close actuarial balance over the succeeding twenty-five years, and if it pursues a fiscal policy that causes any resulting surpluses to increase national saving, active workers will enjoy sufficient increased output to pay for the added costs of these benefits.

Pursuing such a policy would alter the political and economic environment, but it would not eliminate the political difficulties that may arise when future Congresses and presidents must ask workers to bear increased tax burdens to pay for the costs of retirement benefits. The fact that an earlier generation took steps that increased incomes by as much as the future generation is being asked to add to OASDHI outlays will not reduce the transfers that must be made. The political difficulty of making such transfers would probably be influenced in part by the speed with which incomes have risen.

It is important to keep in mind the size of those transfers relative to the increase in consumption that can result from overall economic growth. The cost of the social security program and of social security plus hospital insurance will exceed current levels by a maximum of 1.7 percent and 3.7 percent of net national product, respectively. These maximums will be reached sometime shortly after 2030. If economic growth is robust, these costs will pale beside the increases in income that future cohorts will enjoy; in our view, the costs should not be regarded as significant burdens. The fact that rapid growth of productivity is assumed in official projections, and in our baseline simulation, does not guarantee that it will occur, however. If growth is slow, the added costs of social security and medicare and other benefits to which the elderly are or may become entitled could pose significant burdens for future workers.

As chapter 5 demonstrates, even small variations in productivity are more important for future generations of American workers than is the added burden of increased OASDHI costs. An increase in productivity equal to that assumed in official projections will lead to hourly wages in 2020 equal to twice those in 1986. Growth at the depressed rate of the last fifteen years would leave wages just over 30 percent above those of 1986 (see table 5-4).

In paying for any given set of social security and medicare benefits, the country faces three broad options. One entails building up an OASDHI surplus and using that surplus to increase national saving; a second, building up a surplus and using it to balance deficits elsewhere in the federal budget; and the third option, paying for OASDHI benefits on a pay-as-you-go basis.

Our analysis suggests that option one is the best course to follow because it will bring sizable benefits relative to either of the other options, in the form of increased saving and added output. Total output will be similar under the second and the third options. If the first option proves unsustainable, we favor the third option over the second on distributional grounds. Using OASDHI surpluses to pay for non-OASDHI government activities would entail heavier reliance on payroll taxes and less reliance on personal and corporate income taxes than would option two. The accumulation of large social security surpluses presents a unique opportunity to increase the depressed saving rate of the United States. We think it important to use this opportunity. But if the political system proves unable to forbear from using these surpluses to pay for general activities of government, we would urge a return to pay-as-you-go financing after an adequate contingency reserve has been established.

Changes in Official Actuarial Assumptions, 1986–1988

THE ESTIMATES in this book are based on one of the two intermediate projections—the II-B projections—prepared by the old-age, survivors, and disability insurance actuaries and by the hospital insurance actuaries for the 1986 reports of the OASDI and HI trustees.[1] Both the assumptions and the projection methods used in those reports have been changed. The OASDI and HI trustees modified their demographic and economic assumptions in 1987 and 1988 to reflect new information and changing interpretations of historical trends. This appendix describes some of the most significant changes.

Demographic Assumptions

The optimistic and the intermediate fertility assumptions used in the 1986 reports were quite optimistic in comparison to recent experience. The total fertility rates assumed in 1986 were 2.3 and 2.0, respectively, in the optimistic and intermediate demographic projections (a total fertility rate of 2.11 children per woman is sufficient to maintain a stable population when there is no net immigration). In the 1988 reports, those rates were lowered to 2.2 and 1.9, respectively. The latter rate, which is assumed to be attained in 2012, is only slightly above the total fertility rate observed so far in the 1980s.

More than offsetting the effect of lower assumed fertility in the 1988 reports was the assumption of higher future immigration. In 1986, the assumed rates of net immigration ranged from 700,000

1. *1986 Annual Report of the Board of Trustees of the Federal Old-Age and Survivors Insurance and Disability Insurance [OASDI] Trust Funds* (Baltimore, Md.: Social Security Administration, 1986); and *1986 Annual Report of the Board of Trustees of the Federal Hospital Insurance [HI] Trust Fund* (U.S. Department of Health and Human Services, Health Care Financing Administration, 1986).

immigrants per year, under the optimistic forecast, down to 300,000 per year, under the pessimistic forecast. The intermediate forecast was just 500,000 per year, which is more than 100,000 below the rate of immigration observed over the 1980s.[2] In the 1988 reports, the assumed rates of net immigration were raised to 750,000 immigrants per year under the optimistic projection, 600,000 per year under the intermediate projection, and 450,000 per year under the pessimistic projection. On balance, the new demographic assumptions have a small positive impact on the actuarial balance of the OASDI program, because the favorable effect of higher immigration is more important than the unfavorable effect of lower fertility.

Economic Assumptions

The most problematical aspect of the 1986 projections was the high assumed rate of productivity growth. Output per labor hour was assumed to rise at annual rates of 2.7 percent, 2.4 percent, 2.1 percent, and 1.8 percent, respectively, under the optimistic projection, the two intermediate projections, and the pessimistic projection. Even the lowest assumed rate was well above the actual rate of productivity growth since 1973. In their 1988 reports, the actuaries slashed the productivity assumptions, lowering the assumed rates to 2.3 percent, 2.0 percent, 1.7 percent, and 1.5 percent, respectively. Even under these revised assumptions, however, average productivity is projected to rise faster than it has grown in recent years, although the discrepancy is of course far smaller than it was in the 1986 reports.

Despite the reduced assumed growth in productivity, the rate of growth in covered earnings does not slow under the 1988 assumptions because the work week is forecast to decline at a somewhat slower pace than was assumed in 1986, and the growth in untaxed fringe benefits to proceed at a slower rate. The effects of these two changes nearly offset the impact of slower assumed productivity growth. Whereas taxable earnings per worker were projected to rise 2.5 percent, 2.0 percent, 1.5 percent, and 1.0 percent per year, respectively, under the four economic forecasts prepared in 1986, these growth rates have fallen to 2.4 percent, 1.9 percent, 1.4 percent, and 0.9 percent, respectively, in the same four forecasts prepared in 1988.

The assumptions about future real interest rates are the same in

2. U.S. Bureau of the Census, *Statistical Abstract of the United States, 1988* (GPO, 1987), p. 9.

the 1988 reports as they were in the 1986 reports. Under the intermediate, II-B economic projection, the real interest rate on the trust fund reserves is assumed to reach 2 percent by the year 2000 and remain at that level thereafter.

Effects on Actuarial Balance

The economic and demographic assumptions used in the 1988 reports are more realistic than those used in the 1986 reports, but the overall effect of the revised assumptions on the forecast of actuarial balance is small. For example, under the intermediate, II-B assumptions used in 1986, the OASDI trust funds were expected to experience an income rate of 12.96 percent of taxable payroll and a cost rate of 13.40 percent of taxable payroll. In 1988 (and measured on the same average-cost basis) the combined funds were projected to experience an income rate of 12.95 percent and a cost rate of 13.82 percent.[3] The projected income rate is slightly lower than it was in 1986 and the projected cost rate somewhat higher.

The 1988 deficit is larger than that in 1986 in part because the deficit in the two years 2061 and 2062 added to the projection period is projected to be large. Otherwise, however, the greater pessimism of the economic assumptions is just about offset by the greater optimism of the demographic assumptions. Note that under the average cost method of valuation, the OASDI trust funds have fallen out of close actuarial balance under the II-B assumptions used in the 1988 report. However, under the level financing method that the OASDI trustees adopted in their 1988 report, the combined trust funds remain solvent.

Projections for the hospital insurance trust fund are far more sensitive to changes in economic assumptions than are those of the OASDI trust funds. In particular, the long-term projections for the HI fund have varied widely in recent years because of changes in the assumed growth of hospital costs and use. For example, in 1986 the HI trustees projected that the seventy-five-year average cost rate of the HI fund would be 5.92 percent of taxable payroll under the intermediate, II-B assumptions. In 1988 the II-B projection showed an average seventy-five-year cost rate of 5.25 percent—a decrease of about 11 percent. The short-term outlook has improved even more

3. *1988 OASDI Annual Report*, p. 86.

sharply. Whereas in 1986 the trustees projected that the HI trust fund would be exhausted by 1996, in their 1988 report they projected trust fund depletion by 2005. (Both projections were made using the II-B assumptions.)

The greater sensitivity of the HI projections relative to the OASDI projections reflects the uncertainty of forecasts of future inflation in medical care costs. For that reason, estimates of future HI costs must be taken with a grain of salt. The estimates in this book are based on figures reported in the 1986 HI trustees' report, which are somewhat more pessimistic, though not necessarily more accurate, than those in the 1988 report. Once again, however, it is important to keep in mind that these projections serve only to establish a baseline that we use for calculating the effects of various changes in policy. These calculations would not have changed materially if we had used the 1988, rather than the 1986, projections to establish our baseline.

APPENDIX B

Baseline Model of the Real Economy

FUTURE LABOR SUPPLY is exogenously given in our model by the Social Security Administration's projections of population, labor force participation, unemployment, and average hours of work per year.[1] The future capital stock K in year t is built up as the cumulative sum of past domestic investment I with a constant geometric rate of depreciation δ:[2]

$$(1) \qquad K_t = (1 - \delta) K_{t-1} + I_t.$$

The amount of resources available for domestic investment is just the difference between national saving S and net foreign investment NFI. National saving is the sum of private saving S_p and government saving S_g, which includes the social security surplus S_{ss} as well as net saving in the general fund accounts, S_{gf}. Hence, gross domestic investment is

$$(2) \qquad \begin{aligned} I &= S - NFI \\ &= S_p + (S_{ss} + S_{gf}) - NFI. \end{aligned}$$

We assume that private saving in the future will represent the same, relatively constant fraction of gross national product GNP it has represented throughout the postwar era.[3] The aggregate private saving function is therefore

1. *Economic Projections for OASDHI Cost and Income Estimates, 1986,* Actuarial Study 98 (Baltimore, Md.: Social Security Administration, 1987), pp. 2–15. We did undertake some additional disaggregation into five major sectors, but the labor supply is determined outside of the model and its allocation among the five sectors is not affected by endogenous changes in economic conditions.

2. Different depreciation rates are assumed for structures and equipment. Initial values for the capital stock are derived from data compiled by the Department of Commerce and the Board of Governors of the Federal Reserve. The value of δ was chosen so that the average level of the calculated capital stock was equal to that of the Department of Commerce for the period 1960–1985.

3. We have also experimented with alternative saving functions, in which the private saving rate $\bar{S}$ varies with interest rates, demographic trends, and variations in government saving. Those alternatives are not central to this study (see chapter 5).

(3) $S_p = \bar{s}GNP,$

where the private saving rate $\bar{s}$ is 0.18 over the entire simulation period.

The social security surplus S_{ss} in our baseline simulation is determined by the actuaries' intermediate, II-B projection of revenues and outlays of the old-age, survivors, and disability insurance (OASDI) trust funds. In the baseline projection, however, it is simply included as part of the overall budget, and we assume that the total government budget deficit will eventually fall from its current rate of 3.7 percent of GNP to 1.5 percent of GNP by 1992.[4] This assumption is equivalent to assuming, after 1992, that

(4) $S_{gf} = -0.015 \cdot GNP - \bar{S}_{ss},$

where $\bar{S}_{ss}$ is the actuaries' projection of the social security surplus. The remaining determinant of gross domestic investment in equation 2 is NFI, net foreign investment. In a closed economy,

(5) $NFI \equiv 0.$

(In an open economy NFI will fluctuate, depending on relative rates of return on investment in the United States and abroad.)

Equations 2 through 5 have two implications for saving and domestic investment in the baseline simulation. First, after a transition period lasting from 1986 through 1992, government dissaving becomes a constant share of GNP (-1.5 percent). Second, from 1992 through the end of the projection period, national saving and gross domestic investment are identical and remain a constant share of GNP (16.5 percent).

The entire economy consists of five sectors: nonfarm business, agriculture, government, nonprofit institutions, and private households. The first of these, by far the largest, is treated in greatest detail in our model. Labor and reproducible capital are allocated among sectors in accordance with ratios or observable trends over the postwar period. Output in the nonfarm business sector Y is generated in each year t using labor hours and capital available to that sector, say, L and K. We assume a Cobb-Douglas production function in the nonfarm business sector, implying

(6) $Y_t = A(t) K_t^{\alpha} L_t^{1-\alpha},$

---

4. Over the postwar period, the total federal deficit has averaged about 1.5 percent of GNP.

where α and $1 - \alpha$ are the elasticities of output with respect to capital and labor, respectively, and $A(t)$ is the technical efficiency parameter, which is assumed to grow over time as a result of technical progress. The change in $A(t)$ from year to year measures growth in total factor productivity. In the model α is set to 0.3, the capital income share in the II-B projection, and $A(t)$ is determined so that the baseline projection matches the GNP forecast of the II-B projections. Labor productivity is measured by the ratio Y_t/L_t and rises over time because of increases in $A(t)$ and in capital per worker. Compensation rates w and the gross rate of return on domestic capital r are determined within the nonfarm business sector by the marginal conditions:

(7) $$w = \partial Y/\partial L = (1 - \alpha)(Y/L);$$

(8) $$r = \partial Y/\partial K = \alpha(Y/K).$$

We assume that compensation rates outside the nonfarm business sector (for example, in government) will maintain their historical relationship to those within the nonfarm sector. Hence, real wages in the entire economy are determined by the marginal productivity of labor in nonfarm business.[5]

With a given labor supply and the capital stock generated by equation 1, we can use equations 6 and 7 to derive the technical efficiency parameters $A(t)$ necessary to produce the Social Security Administration's II-B projections of future output and real wages. In the subsequent simulations, $A(t)$ is held constant; variations in investment have no effect on the rate of technical advance. While the II-B productivity assumption, as noted in chapter 4, seems optimistic, it has little effect on our simulations of the effect of changes in saving or in investment on total output.

Representation of Social Security

In addition to a set of equations that predict future saving, investment, output, and the distribution of income among factors of production, we also developed a detailed representation of social

5. Economywide real wage rates do not rise strictly in proportion to marginal productivity in the nonfarm business sector. Other sectors, notably government, are not expected to enjoy productivity gains in the future. Hence, productivity growth in the nonfarm business sector must exceed average real wage growth for the entire economy.

security revenues and outlays. Revenues, disbursements, and reserves in the baseline simulation are calibrated to match the detailed II-B projections of the social security actuaries. Annual revenues consist of payroll taxes, federal income taxes imposed on benefits paid to retirees, and interest on the previous trust fund balance:

$$(9) \qquad\qquad R_{ss} = \tau_{ss}\tilde{w}L + \tau_f\overline{b}B + iF,$$

where R_{ss} is social security revenues, τ_{ss} and τ_f are scheduled payroll and income tax rates, respectively, $\tilde{w}$ is the social-security-covered real wage, $\overline{b}$ is the average real benefit paid to retirees, B is the number of beneficiaries, i is the interest rate payable on the trust fund, and F is the current real fund balance.

The tax rates and the number of beneficiaries are exogenously determined, either by law or by the II-B projections of future labor supply and retirement patterns. The covered wage $\tilde{w}$ is a function of real compensation per hour worked:

$$(10) \qquad\qquad \tilde{w} = f(w).$$

We have used the ratio of covered wages to labor compensation embedded in the II-B projections to produce $\tilde{w}$.[6]

The average real social security retirement benefit $\overline{b}$ is a weighted average of real benefits paid to each surviving age-cohort of retirees. The benefit payable to a cohort of retirees born in the same year is a complicated function that depends largely on the economywide covered real wage when the cohort was sixty years old and the proportions of the cohort that retire at various ages.[7] If t designates the year and a the current age of a given cohort, then $j = t - (a - 60)$ denotes the calendar year in which the cohort turned sixty. In a given calendar year t, the average real benefit $\overline{b}$ payable to a cohort of age a is thus

---

6. This ratio plays a critical role in the projection of the trust fund because fringe benefits are not part of the wage base used to compute social security taxes and benefits. The projected decline of covered wages from 78.6 percent of compensation in 1985 to 63.9 percent in 2060 offsets some of the effects of assuming a rapid growth of labor productivity. *OASDHI Economic Projections, 1986*, p. 122.

7. The formula for the average benefit payable to a cohort of recipients of survivors and disability insurance who begin receiving benefits in the same year is similar. Administrative costs for both programs are proportionate to benefit payments.

(11)
$$\bar{b}_a = b(\tilde{w}_j).$$

The average benefit paid to all retirees is

(12)
$$\bar{b}_t = \sum_{a=62}^{T} \phi_{ta} b(\tilde{w}_j)$$

where sixty-two is the youngest age at which retirement benefits are payable, T is the highest attainable age, and ϕ_{ta} is a weighting factor that reflects the initial size of each cohort as well as its survival rate through age a. These weighting factors are exogenous and ultimately depend on the actuaries' assumptions about birth rates and longevity.

Social security outlays O_{ss} are simply equal to $\bar{b}B$, from which it follows that the social security surplus S_{ss} is equal to $R_{ss} - O_{ss}$. The trust fund balance is equal to the prior year's balance plus the prior year's surplus:

(13)
$$F_t = F_{t-1} + S_{ss,t-1}.$$

The social security actuaries' II-B projection assumes that the real interest rate earned by the trust fund (i in equation 9) will decline from 7.6 percent in 1985 to 2 percent by 1996 and remain constant thereafter. While this assumption is defensible, it is difficult to reconcile with our other baseline assumptions. For example, if the United States is a closed economy and investment follows the pattern implied by equations 2 through 5, the capital-output ratio will rise strongly over the next seventy-five years. In view of the marginal condition in equation 8, the return on capital would be expected to fall over most of the seventy-five-year projection period, not just over the next ten years. If, as generally assumed, the real rate of interest bears some relation to the real rate of return on marginal investment, one would expect the interest rate on the trust fund to decline gradually in proportion to the fall in the marginal product of capital.

To resolve this discrepancy, we assume in our baseline simulation that the real interest rate on the trust fund follows the II-B projection and that the real rate of return on capital is consistent with equation 8. But we also assume that deviations from the baseline in the real after-tax rate of return on capital cause proportional deviations from the baseline in the real interest rate. Thus,

(14)
$$i_t = \theta_t r_t (1 - \tau_c),$$

where τ_c is the corporate tax rate and θ_t is the (exogenous) factor of proportionality required to make equation 14 strictly hold in the baseline simulation. In addition, we use a ten-year average of the after-tax rate of return.

In chapters 4 and 5 we use a concept called incremental burden. In terms of the model, the incremental burden is defined as $(O_{ss,t} - O^*_{ss,t}) - (C_t - C^*_t)$, where $O_{ss,t}$ equals social security outlays in year t, C_t equals consumption in year t, $O^*_{ss,t}$ equals 5.26 percent of baseline NNP, the average for the period 1986 through 1990; and C^*_t is the level of total consumption (private plus public) in the baseline simulation.

Foreign Investment

Under an alternative scenario about the future trend in real interest rates, we relax our assumption that net foreign investment is zero and assume instead that enough saving is invested abroad to leave the net rate of return on domestic capital unchanged over the next seventy-five years. The net return on capital r_n is approximately:

$$(15) \qquad r_n = \frac{\alpha Y - IBT - \delta K}{K}$$

$$= r - \frac{IBT}{K} - \delta,$$

where IBT is indirect business taxes, δK is depreciation (the capital consumption allowance), and r is the gross rate of return. Our assumption regarding the net rate of return is equivalent to setting gross domestic investment, say I^*, so as to maintain[8]

$$(16) \qquad\qquad\qquad r_n \equiv \bar{r}_n,$$

while solving for net foreign investment using identity 2:

$$(17) \qquad\qquad NFI = S - I^*$$

$$= S_p + (S_{ss} + S_{gf}) - I^*.$$

To compute the amount of GNP originating abroad, we assume that the real rate of return on foreign investment is about 20 percent

---

8. This would be equivalent to holding the capital-output ratio fixed if we believed the rates of depreciation δ and indirect business taxation were going to remain constant over the projection period. Since these rates will probably change, the constraint is somewhat more complicated.

TABLE B-1. **Saving Rates, by Age Group**

Age group	Per capita income as a share of average per capita income	Saving rate	Implied weight
16–24	0.35	−0.30	−0.105
25–34	1.02	0.04	0.041
35–44	1.38	0.24	0.331
45–54	1.42	0.32	0.454
55–64	1.28	0.33	0.422
65 and over	0.96	0.28	0.269

Source: Authors' calculations as explained in the text.

greater than the after-corporate-tax real return on domestically invested capital, but that the contribution to U.S. income of a dollar invested abroad relative to capital invested domestically is reduced because foreign taxes on capital income are not part of U.S. gross national product. This is based on the assumption that investors placing their saving abroad would demand a risk premium above the after-corporate-tax rate of return on U.S. investment. The assumption that the premium is equal to 20 percent of the domestic rate of return is obviously somewhat arbitrary. Rates of return on foreign investment have exceeded domestic rates of return over the postwar period. In those simulations that incorporate an assumption of open international capital markets, equations 15, 16, and 17 replace equation 5.

Demographics and Private Saving

In constructing the baseline projections we assumed that the private saving rate would remain constant over the full seventy-five-year projection period. That assumption could be questioned because it is occurring against the backdrop of a major change in the demographic structure of the population.

According to the standard life-cycle model of household behavior, people save during most of their working lives and dissave when young and during retirement. This theory suggests that an increase in the proportion of the population that is aged should reduce national saving by increasing the proportion of dissavers. It also suggests that the U.S. saving rate should currently be rising and that it will fall when the baby-boom generation moves into retirement.

Table B-1 contains estimates of age-specific saving rates and of the distribution of private incomes by age group. The striking aspect of table B-1 is that the saving of the young, not of the old, lies farthest from the overall average.[9] An estimate of the overall saving rate can then be constructed from the following formula:

$$(18) \qquad\qquad s_{pop} = \sum_{j=1}^{n} (p_j/p){\cdot}(y_j/y){\cdot}s_j,$$

where s_{pop} equals the overall saving rate, p equals population, y equals income, and the subscript j refers to a specific age cohort. By holding constant the y_j's and the s_j's it is possible to trace out the influence of changing demographics on the future private saving rate.

The overall private saving rate assumed in the baseline projections is shown in figure B-1, along with two alternatives that show the effect of changing demographic factors. The alternative calculations indicate that as the baby-boom generation ages, the private saving rate should increase. The dominant factor is the decline in the number of young people, not the increase in the number of elderly.

Alternative A uses the weights shown in table B-1. Alternative B lowers the rate for sixty-five- to sixty-nine-year-olds to 0.18, sets the rate at 0.0 at age seventy, and raises the saving rate for sixteen to twenty-four-year-olds from −0.3 to −0.2.[10] Both adjustments indicate that the saving rate will rise as the baby-boom generation matures.

If the elderly are assumed to save nothing, contrary to the survey data in table B-1, alternative B in figure B-1 suggests that the aggregate saving rate would begin to fall early in the twenty-first century. These results suggest that if demographic factors have any effect on private saving, they will induce a cycle in private saving that resembles the accumulation and decumulation of OASDI reserves under current tax rates. In effect, individuals saving for their own retirement will

9. The saving rates are scaled to produce an average private saving rate equal to the 1977–78 average, but the relative pattern follows the saving rates obtained from an average of the 1971–72 and 1980–81 Surveys of Consumer Expenditures. The 1977–78 period was selected as a benchmark because it was not distorted by recession and was near the midpoint of the two surveys. The high saving rate of the retired is consistent with the results of those surveys. In addition, the Social Security Administration analysts distributed corporate saving on the basis of dividend receipts, which are concentrated in the older-age brackets.

10. The resulting estimate of the private saving rate was rescaled to equal the actual rate in 1977–78.

FIGURE B-1. **Actual and Projected Private Saving Rate and Two Alternative Rates, 1950–2060**

Percent of GNP

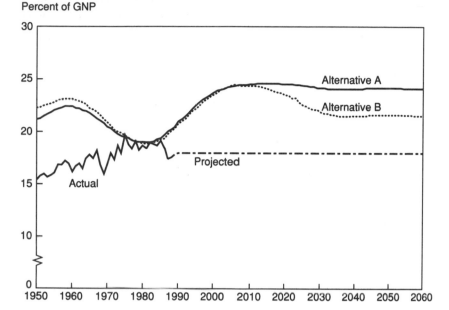

Source: U.S. Department of Commerce, Bureau of Economic Analysis, *United States National Income and Product Accounts,* table 5-1; *Survey of Current Business,* various issues, table 5-1; and authors' calculations as explained in text.

accumulate assets in a pattern similar to the social security system. Such a pattern of behavior would tend to augment saving over the next several decades and reduce the pressures to use the social security surplus for the same purpose.

The historical data, however, lend no support to this projection. Demographic trends appear to bear little relation to past rates of private saving, and in recent years the actual rate has moved in the opposite direction from that predicted. If life-cycle effects were large, the baby-boom demographic bulge should have depressed private saving in the 1960s and 1970s.[11] In fact, saving did not fall. Nor did the private saving rate increase in the 1980s as the baby-boom

11. Several research studies have attempted to include demographic variables in statistical studies of private saving behavior in the postwar period, but the influence of these variables appears to be small. Charles Lieberman and Paul Wachtel, "Age Structure and Personal Saving Behavior," in George M. von Furstenberg, *Social Security versus Private Saving* (Cambridge, Mass.: Ballinger, 1979), pp. 315–57.

generation matured; instead, it declined. Either the effects of demographic events on saving were small or other factors overwhelmed them. On balance, we believe that no solid evidence justifies abandoning Denison's Law. We therefore assume that future private saving rates will remain relatively constant.

Index